Remember and Do Not Forget

*Rabbinic Testimonies
of January 6, 2021:
A Horrific Day
in American History*

edited by
Rabbi Menachem Creditor
and Rabbi Jesse Olitzky

foreword by Ruth Messinger

Remember and Do Not Forget

2021 Paperback Edition, *First Printing*
© 2021 by Menachem Creditor and Jesse Olitzky
Foreword © 2021 by Ruth Messinger

ISBN: 9798592895869

לֹא תַעֲמֹד עַל־דַּם רֵעֶךָ אֲנִי יְהֹוָה
**You shall not stand idly by
when the life of another is in danger.
I am God.**

Leviticus 19:16

**Over and above personal problems,
there is an objective challenge to
overcome inequity, injustice,
helplessness, suffering, carelessness,
and oppression.**

Rabbi Abraham Joshua Heschel

**A time comes when
silence is betrayal.**

Rev. Dr. Martin Luther King

Remember and Do Not Forget

CONTENTS

Foreword

January 6, 2021
Ruth Messinger

We are in an extraordinary and challenging moment, one so much more critical than even the extended challenge we have been in for close to a year. Of course, our larger context has been an ongoing health pandemic and a consequent economic crisis and to the fact that the pandemic has exposed severe racial fault lines in health care and the fact that we have seen horrendous recent explosions of race-based violence — facts I continue to believe we must address.

But those continuing challenges don't speak to where we find ourselves after the events of January 6, 2021.

I am a product of time and events, deeply moved and shaken by what has occurred in our country. It shapes my remarks and makes them more raw and more intense than my hosts or I might have intended.

So, please, take a deep breath. Really. And let's look at the good news and the bad news.

First, the election in Georgia. Regardless of which candidates you might have supported, a run-off election in which the turn out was almost as high as in the general election, in which an unprecedented number of young people participated, in which the State will send to Washington its first Black Senator, a distinguished pastor, and its first Jewish Senator, a man steeped in his own traditions, is worthy of note and of celebration!

It is for sure a tribute to the importance of protecting the voting rights of every person in this country, making it easier not harder to cast a vote, and we know how much work that requires in WI, in NY, in GA—just about every place. And it is a tribute to the power of grassroots organizing and coherent leadership, provided most visibly in this instance by Stacy Abrams.

A positive marker for our democracy. And yet, at the same time, you—and we— had the aftermath of the shooting in Kenosha and the renewed need for the nation to focus on gun violence, police-community relations, police accountability and the capacity of our criminal justice systems to deal with this and similar episodes.

And then came January 6, 2021 which already feels several years ago. A moment in which angry crowds were urged to march on our Capitol, by our President; in which—and again I am really striving here for the maximum degree of objectivity I can muster—a physical citadel and symbol of our two hundred-and-fifty-year-old democracy was under siege, terrorists destroyed property, lives were lost, and our elected representatives were in real physical danger.

During this attempted coup the attackers brought not only weapons but confederate flags, giant crosses and Nazi imagery into the capitol building; organized around their belief in white supremacy; and at least one elected official and several demonstrators evoked Hitler as a leader and some demonstrators wore tee shirts with disgusting anti-Semitic messages.

It now seems clear - and clearly absurd - that there was inadequate or perhaps no preparation by the Capitol police and other enforcement officers for what was certainly likely to occur and that nothing these officials did bore ANY relationship to how we have seen police respond to demonstrations throughout this country by people of color.

The National Guard was not called in nearly soon enough, a decision that can be traced to the White House's chain of command. We had yet another dramatic example — not that we needed one — of the dangerous double standard that prevails in our country.

We will need to process these events — Georgia, Kenosha, Washington — in your own ways, sometimes agreeing and sometimes disagreeing, but the overarching commitment must be shared, spoken in many ways, at many times in our history, here as articulated by a life hero of mine: Rabbi Abraham Joshua Heschel. He wrote, "In a free society where terrible wrongs exist, some are guilty, but all are responsible."

Fifteen words, but that is my mantra and my message. The privilege of living in a democracy, the privilege of no longer being an enslaved people, the further privilege for some of us of our whiteness, or our professional position, or our economic standing or our citizenship or our access to resources is that we must acknowledge our responsibility and commit to action.

We have texts. We actually have texts galore — in the Torah, in rabbinic commentary, in parsha analyses, in contemporary writings, from people of other faiths — telling us we must act, we must lean in, we must do the actual work of pursuing justice.

Back to Heschel. What does it mean to accept responsibility? It may be that no one reading these words is a person charged with the training of our various police forces, but we all know it is an issue. We are not, most of us, in charge of making health care less racist — at least not directly. To go even further down this road, many of us who said we were shocked by the events of January 6, 2021 — and we were — also knew at some level that things were getting increasingly dangerous.

We may not have caused any or all of these problems, but we are not free to ignore them. We have an obligation to be upstanders, not bystanders, to figure out why and how to take responsibility and act for our own and for the greater good. We need to look into the root causes of the problems that are defining our era and consider the myriad ways in which we can and must be involved as individuals and as Jews in the ongoing struggles for justice and equity.

We do live in a democracy or, as Ben Franklin said when asked if the founding fathers were building a republic or a monarchy, "A republic, if you can keep it." That is our job, dramatically after this week. What do we need to do to keep and to improve this republic, to never again see threatened our historic commitment to a peaceful transfer of power?

It is our job to protect this republic. To me, that means "leaning in", acknowledging our role in strengthening voting rights, picking elected officials who we believe will engage directly on making social change on our behalf, sticking with unpopular causes and organizing with others in our shul community, in our other organizations to pursue the changes that are needed. It means listening to and learning from others what safeguards are not in place that should be and organizing to create those.

There will be LOTS of choices, and we cannot do it all, nor can we retreat to the convenience of being overwhelmed. What we cannot do, most particularly, is say that January 6, 2021, was an aberration, and it won't happen again. That would be forfeiting on the responsibilities that Franklin and Heschel told us to take up.

Even the Torah portion for the week that coincided with the attack speaks to these issues in multiple ways. In it, we see Moshe standing up for others, Jews and non-Jews. But we also see him being asked by God to lean in, to take leadership responsibility, and he is more than reluctant, turning down the request many times — because he knows, as do each of you, that it is going to be hard, not always rewarding, and for sure that it will be slow going.

Ultimately, he accepts responsibility and, guess what - that is not ever easy. That is why we each of us needs to find our niche, create our self-care and support systems, educate and organize with others and become organizers with resilience, determination and a good dose of moral courage.

One other parsha note: We read this week that Moses saw the burning bush. But commentators point out that it is not just that he saw the bush; he saw that it was on fire and was not being consumed. That is when he realized that it was no ordinary bush, that there was a divine force involved. So too, must we pay more attention to what is happening around us — not just "see" it, but strive to give it more than passing attention, to understand what the events of our week or our year have to tell us.

The tradition, taken together, tells us over and over that this is our responsibility. To see, to learn from what we see, to act because we have the capacity to make the world a better place, to make informed change because we can.

I want before I close to consider one text. People sometimes suggest that I am picking from Heschel or Elie Wiesel or Dr King and pursuing my own 21st century version of urging others to help heal the world. So let me share the wise words of a famous Torah commentary:

> "If a person of learning participates in public affairs and serves as judge or arbiter, they give stability to the land...But if they sit in their home and say to themselves, 'What have the affairs of society to do with me? ...Why should I trouble myself with the people's voices of

protest? Let my soul dwell in peace!'—if one does this, they overthrow the world."[1]

Before the world is overthrown, we need to get to work. And the good news is we are meeting at a time when the days are getting longer, when there is more light coming into our lives. We need that light, and we need to share it with others, maximizing the opportunities for all of us to move toward justice.

---

[1] Midrash Tanchuma, Mishpatim 2

Introduction

Rabbi Menachem Creditor
and Rabbi Jesse Olitzky

It has been said that journalism is the "first draft of history," reporting in the immediate aftermath of events. But with the passage of time, historical recording and interpretations of the same events often shift. As rabbis, we are trained to appreciate not only history, but also *historiography*, the study of historical writing. It is therefore important beyond words to find the right ones to point to pivotal moments in time, and to remember.

We are told in the Torah to both "*zachor et asher lecha Amalek*," to remember the Amalekites, and "*timcheh et Zecher Amalek*," erase the memory of the Amalekites. The juxtaposition of these two commands create a tension. We are meant to remember and not forget, to erase the memory of Amalek but not let that memory nor its erasure entirely define us. We remember so that we can use our collective history to shape our future.

There is great power in memory, arguably a blessing and a curse that God has given us. Truly to remember is to relive. We might choose to relive joyful moments again and again, but we also remember darker moments, for those also shape us as a society and define who we are.

We will remember the events of January 6, 2021. We also understand that, just like Torah, there is power in collective memory. This is especially true considering that we may remember the events of this day differently, each of us reflecting on it using our own eyes, hearts – and our unique choices of words.

Was the attack on the United States Capitol on January 6, 2021 a riot? A coup? Insurrection? Domestic terrorism? A protest? Words matter, and how we remember is shaped by the words we use. As the great essayist and thinker George Orwell once observed:

> "Political language is designed to make lies sound truthful and murder respectable, and to give an appearance of solidity to pure wind."

We have done our best to collect diverse rabbinic testimonies from an indescribable moment of American history with a commitment to remember and a promise to not forget. We will not be defined by the threats of white supremacists and the acts of domestic terrorists. But they undoubtedly shape us and shape our view of the world.

We are not ignorant enough to think that bigotry did not exist before the Trump era nor would we be so foolish as to suggest that it will cease once that era is over. But we had thought that American society was in collective agreement that bigotry belonged in the sewers and gutters of society. But when the President amplified such bigotry in 240-characters at a time on his Twitter feed for four years straight, and worse yet, successfully used that bigotry to influence his supporters, he gave them permission to proudly and loudly -- *and violently* -- express such hateful bigotry for the world to see and incite violence. We are not ignorant enough to believe that Amalek has ceased to exist. But it is our deepest prayer that as long as we remember, as long as we continue to call out the events of this dark day for what they are, then the bigotry of Amalek will return to the sewers of society, where it belongs.

Rabbi Menachem Creditor
Rabbi Jesse Olitzky

Tevet 5781
January 2021

To Truly Heal as A Nation, We Must Have a Deep National Reckoning

Rabbi Sharon Brous

When it became clear that the Rev. Raphael Warnock, pastor of Ebenezer Baptist Church, had just been elected the first Black senator from the state of Georgia, he addressed the nation, quoting Psalm 30:6: "We may lie down weeping in the night, but joy comes in the morning."

That was hours before the violent insurrection began at the Capitol building, incited by the president and designed to disrupt the certification process that would cement President-Elect Joe Biden's win.

We are deep in the dark night. Representatives hid under desks and prayed. Congressional staffers claimed they had never experienced anything more terrifying. Five people are dead. Our nation is reeling.

We will not arrive at the joyous morning the Psalmist promises unless we're honest about how we got where we are.

No part of this fevered coup attempt was accidental, nor should it be surprising.

Many Americans have been fed a steady diet of racist lies for generations. They've been raised on the heresy that God loves them more. They've been taught that they will be diminished in a more just, equitable and compassionate America. They've become intoxicated by the lie of white supremacy, a spiritual cancer that has become metastasized

17

at the heart of their movement. They've been taught that patriotism requires the suppression, criminalization and dehumanization of fellow citizens.

As the riots unfolded, I felt the weight of all these heresies bearing down on our nation's soul. Watching Capitol police clear barriers to grant insurrectionists entry into the building, I felt a rising sense of fear, but it was not the fear that they'd succeed. Everyone knew this was an ill-fated coup attempt before it began. It was the fear that we'd collectively move on too quickly once it ended.

We can't treat this as a dangerous anomaly. We cannot usher in the new dawn until we name, address and eradicate the pernicious forces that normalized this toxicity over generations so it could erupt as it did this week.

Who is responsible?

Not only those who so brazenly threatened and stormed and broke glass, and not only those who egged them on from the Senate floor, though they surely must be held accountable.

But their culpability is shared by every person who silently stood by as the lies festered and the violence was fueled. By all those who dismissed the overt embrace of far-right groups by our president, those who shrugged when terrorists stormed the statehouse and plotted to kidnap the governor of Michigan, those who demurred when children were separated from their families at the border, and those who cried "law and order!" when peaceful Black Lives Matter protesters were targeted and tear-gassed, beaten and brutalized. Those who engaged in homiletical acrobatics to muddy the abundantly clear "fine people on both sides," and those who said, again and again, "I don't like what he says, but I like what he does." Those who justified, excused, obfuscated and pointed fingers at everyone but the architects of the machinery of fear and division that is breaking our nation.

My fear was not that the insurrectionists would win, but that we'd all lose — because we lack the will to engage in a real reckoning, to write a new narrative, a shared redemption story for America.

There's no shortcut here. It's not only the recklessness, fecklessness and shocking criminality of the president and his enablers that got us here. Silence and complicity are also sins. Either we work to dismantle oppressive systems, or our inaction becomes the mortar that sustains them.

In times like these, the vision of a just and loving multiracial democracy may seem fantastical or even farcical. We have to remember that "joy comes in the morning."

We can transform the tearful night into a joyous morning. I believe this to be possible. To bring on the new dawn, we'll have to be visionary, steadfast and fiercely principled.

We have to remember, the deepest darkness is the moment just before the dawn. The contours of the joyous morning we yearn for will be shaped by the boldest and most imaginative dreams we allow ourselves to dream from within the weepy night. This is no end; it's a new beginning.

After an Insurrection at the Capitol

Rabbi Aaron Brusso

5 years ago in February of 2016 I offered this interpretation of the story of the Golden Calf:

> The Torah says "Moses saw that the people were out of control since Aaron had let them get out of control so that they were a menace to any who might oppose them."
>
> The word for letting them get out of control in Hebrew is *farua*. It is a curious word, but an important verb in that it may explain what Aaron did wrong. The commentator Rashi explains that *farua* means *meguleh*, that Aaron uncovered or revealed the people's base, menacing nature. It was there, but Aaron provided the permission and license for it to come out in force.
>
> The commentator Rashbam thinks *farua* means that Aaron gave them permission to reject laws and norms that served to restrain their behavior. All seem to agree that Aaron was an enabler.
>
> There seems to be a fundamental goal of leadership being promoted here: helping people to manage their worst tendencies in order to be the best they can be.
>
> What if a different kind of leader had been at the helm when the people gathered to demand a god? What if Korach was there instead of Aaron? Korach is the one who challenged Moses and asked "isn't everyone holy? Why do you put yourself above us?" Korach was a populist. Of Korach the rabbis say: "disagreements can be for principles, for the sake of heaven, but Korach's

disagreement was not based on principle, it was not for the sake of heaven."

What if Korach's response was: "I hear you're frustrated with Moses. I'm not surprised. You know I don't think he understands us." Someone from the crowd might then have shouted: "he grew up in pharaoh's palace." To which Korach might have responded: "Did you hear what he said? Wow. Say that again. You mean he might not really be an Israelite? Whoa. I'm not saying that, you are, but I do think it's worth checking into."

Up until now, the Israelites have been powerless and Moses it seems has been calling all the shots. This shift towards scrutiny of Moses' legitimacy feels suddenly empowering.

"What I have noticed," Korach might then have continued, "is that Moses has some trouble getting his words out." To which the crowd would knowingly laugh. Sensing the swelling support Korach might be emboldened to say "Let my people g-g-g-g-go." To which the crowd would roar with laughter.

What a relief. For so long they have felt only fear and confinement and now they feel a bit liberated, free to express something they've kept inside. Korach has made it ok for them to laugh at something that polite manners had taught them not to.

Korach might then turn to *the erev rav*. Torah explains that the Israelites, left Egypt with a "mixed multitude". The *erev rav* were other nations who were enslaved by Pharaoh and achieved freedom at the same time as the Israelites. The Exodus was not about tribal freedom, it was about human freedom.

"You know there are people here who came out of Egypt with us and I'm not really sure how that happened,"

Korach might say. "What permission did they have?" "Do we really know who they are?" The crowd so long used to feeling the subject of subjugation would revel in the feeling of us with a say of what should happen to them.

Korach would be careful not to come across as too negative. He would realize the need to be seen as likable. "Joshua," he might say, referring to the leader who brings the Israelites into the land of Canaan, "Joshua, he loves me. We get along great. Very likable guy."

It is these moments of acting the "good guy" that purchase Korach license to say about a person in the crowd who is questioning his approach "I'd like to punch him in the face." The Israelites are not used to leaders speaking so openly, boldly, and brashly. It feels real, authentic, and liberating of their own base feelings.

Korach is not a leader; he is a demagogue. He has the instincts of how to leverage the feelings of a crowd. He feels none of the shame that most of us feel that hold us back from this kind of behavior.

The Torah uses the word *farua* to describe how Aaron enabled the Israelites to unleash. And there's a reason. *Farua* sounds like Pharaoh. Pharaoh is not a person, Pharaoh is a base instinct that exists in all of us. It is the moment when a crowd turns into a mob. When a human being turns into an animal. It is a feeling of freedom that is predicated on subjugation. It can come across as laughter and fraternal feeling but it's not funny. It's dangerous.

We have seen people throughout history who do such things. They are often initially written off as marginal, not serious, celebrities seeking attention. A tipping point comes and suddenly this person is not so marginal. They are mainstream. We can't believe our kids have to be exposed to the language and the behavior. We are not sure how it happened.

Freedom from slavery in Egypt was not meant to free us from controlling our language, free us from controlling our hate, or free us from controlling our base instincts.

Only the demagogue frees us to do that. And in a cruel twist of irony we see how freedom can actually lead us back to Pharaoh.

I offered those words 5 years ago in February 2016.

At the time, and since, people said, "ignore what he says and pay attention to what he does. It's about the policy not the prose."

We now know with certainty that is not true.

And if we didn't know it a week ago, we saw the danger with our own eyes on Wednesday when the demagogue incited a mob to insurrection and defilement of our Capitol. Words matter.

People found common cause with this demagogue since some of their interests were being met. A month after I gave that sermon I attended the AIPAC policy conference where the demagogue spoke as a candidate for president. A top AIPAC leader met with rabbis the night after he spoke. The AIPAC leader acknowledged that what the demagogue had been saying was very troubling. And then the AIPAC leader said "but at least in his speech today he landed on our side of the field."

I couldn't believe it.

Jews had suffered for thousands of years being on the other side of that equation when people would say, "At least he's good for us; we are not the Jews."

I spoke up at this rabbinic gathering and said to the AIPAC leader: "if he is a danger to others, it is not good enough that he lands on our side of the field. It's not good enough." There is no common cause with a demagogue. The risk is that we normalize and enable something very dangerous.

And about denying the results of this election…

One of my jobs as clergy is to help people mourn losses, to face and specifically name the loss. To sit with it and describe it so that it can be let go. Without that necessary process we get hung up in the past. We bring expectations forward with us into a future that will not meet them. And we compound our feelings of disappointment.

It is a sacred role I am honored to play as clergy. People place their losses in my hands and I hold them with great care. I let them know that I see them and that they are not alone. We all have losses we have to mourn and we can't move on until we do.

It is a titanic responsibility. People are sharing their vulnerabilities. They are opening themselves up. These are moments in which, if not handled carefully, much damage can be done.

People are susceptible to being convinced they have been cheated. As a result, they should be angry for something was stolen from them. They should not see it as a loss, but as something taken by a malevolent force.

If there is nothing to litigate or if all that could be litigated has been, anything done to lend validity to and perpetuate these inclinations is nothing short of emotional manipulation and malpractice.

The role of helping people to face, name, let go, and move on from losses is not the job of clergy alone. It is a role we all can play for people in our life. But it is especially important in its symbolic power when practiced by leaders. Whole societies can be brought through a mourning process and emerge on the other side as more mature versions of themselves.

Alternatively and most devastatingly, societies can be manipulated at their most vulnerable to nurse and deepen their grievances over loss convinced that things can be reversed.

A leader who does this does not feel the sacred responsibility of holding another human being's hopes, dreams, and losses in their hands.

We see what happens when you don't let people mourn. They destroy their own Temple.

Mitt Romney who has emerged as a true statesman and wise leader said: "the best way we can show respect for the voters who are upset is by telling them the truth. That is the burden, and the duty, of leadership."

We have much to learn from all of this but one Jewish teaching sums it up: "words create worlds." We must choose our words and the leaders who speak them wisely.

Ken yehi ratzon - may it be so.

I Never Felt as Strongly About the Prayer for the Government as I Did Today

Rabbi Menachem Creditor

I remember many years ago feeling ambivalent about the prayer for the government recited in synagogues every Shabbat morning. Were we sanctifying the policies of an administration? What of political leaders who would use religious language in pursuit of their particular agendas? I wondered: Isn't God bigger than that?

My feelings have changed as I've grown older, but never have I prayed as deeply for the government of the United States as I did today upon witnessing a violent mob attack our nation's capital. Professional journalists and smartphone-wielding citizens have made clear that we are in dire need of heaven's help.

As I type, my heart is trembling. My children have asked me to explain the inexplicable, and my response has been a worried, stumbling prayer: Please God, protect our government's leaders, who have been whisked away from the very heart of America because of the threat of physical harm.

Regardless of a citizen's political commitments regarding small government or universal healthcare, fiscal conservatism or foreign policy, the ancient sage Rabbi Chanina, the deputy high priest of his day, defined what it means to pray for the government when he said:

> "One should pray for the welfare of the government, as were it not for the fear of the government, every person would swallow their neighbor alive."

Today's despicable violence in Washington, D.C., proved him right.

The common good is a fragile thing, and its preservation depends upon the collective stewardship of our leaders. Jewish history is replete with examples of how easy it can be for a leader to incite societal fissures. Just this week we read in the Torah of Pharaoh's successful method of incremental dehumanization of our ancestors, fomenting a division between us (Israelites) and them ("real" Egyptians). Jews have learned to trust the Psalmist who warned not to place eternal "trust in princes or kings." But we have also learned to ask heaven's help in appointing leaders who will act in good trust. In other words, we pray that our government will succeed at keeping faith with the people it is called to serve.

The desecration of America's national symbols today, the wielding of weapons on the Congress floor, the assault on law enforcement and the leaders they are sworn to protect is not only the action of a riotous mob; it was nothing less than an assault on the health of our country, an act of American blasphemy.

A faithful person, according to the great American civil rights leader Rabbi Abraham Joshua Heschel, "holds God and man in one thought at one time, at all times, who suffers harm done to others, whose greatest passion is compassion, whose greatest strength is love and defiance of despair."

When a Jew beseeches God to protect the government, it isn't a partisan prayer or the expectation that God will explicitly intervene in a historical moment. A prayer for the government is a kind of citizen's Hippocratic Oath. We pledge to protect each other from harm.

This prayer is a traditional commitment to society's welfare, a ritualized way of ingraining in the collective Jewish conscience the biggest command of all: loving our neighbors as ourselves.

So let us pray.

Teach Your Children

Rabbi Nicole Guzik

Like many of you, my heart shattered as I watched the insurrection at the US Capitol. News blaring in the background, tears streaming down my face, I thought, "What am I teaching my children?" As a collective society blessed to live in this beautiful country, what are we teaching our children? As a rabbi who beseeches God daily to extend heaven's peace onto this earth, what do our children need to hear and glean from this very moment? From this year? Through this trauma and ravaged emotional state?

And so, to my children, I will teach:

> ~You are safe in my arms and I will do everything in my power to protect you. But as human beings, as Jews, we must stand together and ensure that same privilege of safety for every child of God.

> ~You have a right to use your voice. But to always remember, words hold the power to create and likewise, hold the power to destroy. Use your words to build worlds, create sacred connections, and lift souls. Let your voice be a beacon of light.

> ~You are better than the images of hate and destruction displayed across our screens. Use your hands for moments of embrace. Channel your anger and rage through acts of loving-kindness. Choose role models that engage in civil dialogue and productive conversation. Seeks paths that lead to understanding.

~You plant the seeds for a better tomorrow. My children, as much as we want to close our eyes at this dark moment in history, widen your gaze. Remember, you are the change-makers. You are the bearers of peace. Observe. Feel. Absorb. Learn. But then my precious babies, with determination and persistence, fight for a brighter future - for yourself and for generations to come.

According to the Midrash, the angels questioned and interrogated God in the decision to create human beings. God gave a convincing rebuttal, remarking on the human being's wisdom and intellect. And even though the traditional text seems to highlight humanity's mental discernment, I implore all of us to teach our children that true wisdom is paired with the heart. We inherit a world in which too often, our hearts remain closed, shut off, and disengaged with that which seems frightening or different.

Open those eyes. Open those hearts. I will teach my children to always, be worthy of their creation.

Democracy and Torah

Rabbi David Wolkenfeld

This past Wednesday afternoon, I spoke to a group of students who attend a Christian high school that is a sort of Protestant version of the Jewish day schools that many of our children attend. In between their semesters, they had enrolled in a week-long course exploring the broader context of their own Christian faith. They had never been to a synagogue. They had never spoken to a rabbi before. Their knowledge of Judaism was mostly gleaned from what they knew from the Bible. I love speaking to audiences like that. It's a creative challenge to summarize all of Judaism in ten minutes to teenagers with little prior background. And, as I've shared before, I find the questions that they ask to be absolutely unpredictable and absolutely fascinating.

One student asked me if Jews ever had disagreements about matters of religious practice or ritual and, if we did, how have we resolved those disputes. So that gave me a chance to share with them that, indeed, Jews don't always agree about matters of religious practice or ritual, or matters of philosophy or worldview, and that our sacred tradition is, in large part, a record of our disagreements and debates. And because we debate and analyze and try to prove the correctness of our positions by using words and arguments and discourse, we have survived through the centuries of our exile with our portable homeland that is renewed each generation by our continued commitment to study Torah, argue about its meaning and implications, and then live our lives according to our best understanding of what we are meant to do. Sometimes disputes are resolved, but never by compulsion or force, only when one side of a debate convinces the Jewish people that its path is correct, until a time arises when another option may become dominant.

I left the students and noticed some alarmed text messages from family. Only then did I see for the first time the images that had shocked and appalled men and women of good will across the country and across the world. There is a deliberate grandeur to Washington DC, no place more so than the Capitol building. That grandeur is meant to evoke a certain awe and reverence for the democratic process itself through which each one of us is represented. So many men and women whom I admire have worked and debated and legislated in the halls of congress on behalf of human welfare and freedom. It was a profound sense of violation to see the confederate battle flag, the banner of treason and hate, being waved in the United States capitol. It is a source of burning anger to know that the riot was inspired and encouraged by powerful politicians, including the President himself, who riled up an angry mob, and then cowardly sent them on without him to spread havoc and violence. And it is frightening to be reminded of how our country sits at the very precipice of political violence that can threaten the safety of members of congress acting on our behalf, and can easily and quickly threaten our safety as well.

Fear of anarchic violence and fear of the replacement of democratic deliberation by mob rule, are rightfully contained by the fear and reverence for the authority that effective government can inspire. Rabbi Chanina, deputy to the High Priest said, in Pirkei Avot, "one should pray for the welfare of the government - for were it not the fear that the government instills, each individual would swallow up their neighbors alive."

The government that Rabbi Chanina knew was Rome. And, as the *sgan kohen*, the perpetual deputy High Priest, Rabbi Chanina was presumably passed over, time and again, for a promotion that he deserved, to become the High Priest. (Those of us learning *daf yomi* learned just a few weeks ago that Rabbi Chanina was the most qualified expert on the intricate laws of purity needed to be an excellent high priest). Yet, he never entered the Holy of Holies on Yom Kippur and he never served in a position of full religious authority because a despotic foreign-imposed government did not want him in that role. But even that despotic foreign-imposed government was preferable to anarchy and the struggle of "all against all." We have seen a small glimpse this week into what it looks like when there is no fear or reverence for governmental authority and when the orderly transition of power is replaced by a violent struggle of all against all to determine how power will be wielded, by whom, and for how long.

But this fear or reverence for established authority is not the only fear I have been contemplating.

Parashat Shemot opens with a description of the rapid decline in status of the Hebrews in Egypt. In just a few words the Torah describes the descent from the generation of *Yosef* and his brothers, who were honored in Egypt, to slavery, oppression, and the murder of Hebrew babies. The first spark of redemption that halts and diverts this tragic story is the resistance of two midwives, Shifra and Puah, to Pharaoh's murderous plans. Shifra and Puah, the Torah tells us "feared God - and because they feared God they were not afraid of Pharaoh and they spared the Jewish boys."

Between these two poles of reverence - reverence for government and reverence for God – is the entire framework for democratic self-government. Stable self-government, in which the peaceful transfer of power is itself revered, even by those who are overlooked for leadership like Rabbi Chanina, endures precisely because there is a way to perpetuate government from one leader to the next. And, stable self-government requires citizens with moral backbone and moral clarity. Sometimes a midwife has to say no to a great king.

Four years ago, on *Parashat Shemot*, I spoke to you about the complicated relationship between religious Jews and democratic freedoms. I shared that when Napoleon marched into Russia as a flawed standard-bearer of liberty, equality, and brotherhood, he faced the spiritual opposition of the *Ba'al HaTanya*, the first Lubavitcher Rebbe, who argued that the cruelty and oppression of the Russian czar would bind the Jewish people to God and to the Torah whereas the freedoms represented by Napoleon would alienate us from God and the Torah. Two centuries later we know that the *Ba'al HaTanya* might have been correct to reject Napoleon, but he was wrong about the political circumstances in which Judaism thrives.

Democracy is good for Jews and good for Judaism because it requires the cultivation of character and that is a project we should embrace and a business we invented. Democracy is good for Jews and good for Judaism because resolving disputes and transferring power from one set of hands to another by deliberation and debate instead of violence, is the most sustainable and reliable method humans have discovered to cultivate stability and continuity. The Roman Republic is one possible model for modern democratic self-government. Athenian democracy is another possible model for modern Democratic self-government. But neither of those models lasted a very long time. But the culture of the *beit midrash* represents another ancient, enduring, and still vital model for democratic self-government.

Our method for debating and deciding matters of the utmost importance - *devarim ha'omdim b'rumo shel olam* - without recourse to force or violence, but only through deliberation, debate, and discourse, has ensured our survival for thousands of years. A similar commitment has led to peace and freedom in the nations of the world that have adopted those methods for resolving their disputes. That has been this country's greatest strength, and with our renewed commitment to democracy, it can be so again.

As the tide turns in favor of redemption in *Parashat Shemot* the Torah presents one redemptive moment after another, each one necessary but not sufficient to conclusively launch our freedom. Shifra and Puah had to resist Pharaoh's command to murder Hebrew babies. Moshe, leaving the palace to spend the day with his erstwhile Egyptian brothers, had to somehow understand that his true brothers were the Hebrew slaves he had been observing, and expresses his solidarity with them and with us. But the final shift towards redemption occurs when the Hebrew slaves, at long last, after generations of suffering and degradation call out to God:

> A long time after that, the king of Egypt died. The Israelites were groaning under the bondage and cried out; and their cry for help from the bondage rose up to God.

The *Netziv* points out that this turning point in human history was sparked by our decision to gather and to pray. It does not say that we cried out to God while we were working, but rather that we cried out to God, in a collective voice and in an organized way in response to our bondage.

And this is my final request to you today. When frightening and tragic events occurred in recent years, I had the ability to find comfort in the community that we create when we gathered for prayer here in our shul. I had faith that our prayers were heard, and I knew that even if they would not be answered, at least I stood among good people who were sensitive to that which was wrong or tragic in the world and that too was a source of strength. While we lack the capacity to gather in one place in prayer in large numbers, I ask you to connect your *tefilot* in the coming days to the fears and the hopes that we feel as Jews and that we feel as Americans. Our neighbors and friends are falling victim to a deadly pandemic that is still increasing in scope - yesterday saw the record number of COVID deaths so far. Our neighbors and friends are worried about their jobs and their ability to provide for their basic needs and those of their families. And our fellow citizens need some help in learning how to argue and debate without violence and without hatred.

A Call for Moral Clarity

Rabbi Ezra Schwartz

There is no need for yet another voice to come forward and talk about how despicable Wednesday's attempted putsch was. There is no need for someone else to speak about the awfulness that the current occupant of the Oval Office brought about. I hope that those with more sway in the larger American community, from both sides of the aisle, will speak forcefully about this. However, whether or not they do so is not my concern.

My concern is for my community. Sadly, there is a genuine need to address those closest to me, people I *daven* (pray) with and with whom I share a commitment to Torah, *mitzvos* (Jewish commandments) and traditional morality. There is a need to address the Orthodox Jews who participated in the rally, those who celebrated the event even silently, those who sympathized with its goals if not with its implementation, and even those who in their Monday morning quarterbacking fell short of voicing uncompromised condemnation of the entire event. In short, what happened on Wednesday should force our community to recalibrate our moral compass and take careful stock of whether we are being true to *hashkafas ha'Torah* (the outlook of the Torah). I believe that the event needs to be reacted to with the strongest possible condemnation.

Let's think about some of the imagery from the event. We saw not only the disruption of Congress and the desecration of our halls of government, we also saw Confederate and Nazi flags raised; symbols of hatred, oppression, and murder proudly flown in the halls of our government. But most disturbing of all we were witness to at least one Israeli flag flying next to these most odious symbols. Wednesday's attempted putsch runs counter to all the values *Degel Yisrael* (the Jewish flag) represents. The Israeli flag stands for thousands of years of longing for freedom. *Degel Yisrael* should be a modern articulation of a prophetic promise; that *Klal Yisrael* (the Jewish people) will rise from slavery and oppression and champion the values of justice articulated by the *Neviim* (prophets) to the entire world. *Degel Yisrael* proudly flies against the hateful symbols of Confederacy and Naziism. It certainly has no place being flown in tandem with these most putrid symbols of hatred and oppression. Moving the embassy may have been very positive, peace with our Arab brethren is certainly wonderful; but for that *nezid adashim*, for that bowl of lentils, we cannot give up on the true meaning of *Degel Yisrael* and moral place *Medinat Yisrael* was founded to represent.

More than that, I am sickened by the image of my brothers and sisters, people wearing *yarmulke* (skullcaps) and *tzitzis* (ritual fringes), skirts and snoods, who were not embarrassed to align themselves with the most vulgar parts of America. I cannot fathom how Jews, *Shomrei Torah u'mitzvos* (observant of the Torah and its commandments), stand arm in arm with those wearing sweatshirts that state 6 Million Were not Enough. How can anyone with a beating Jewish heart march arm in arm with those who wear shirts glorifying Auschwitz?

I am deeply disturbed that so many in my community, even if they did not join in person, were sympathetic to the cause and therefore unwilling to condemn the rally even after we witnessed the desecration it brought forth. I am pained to read supposed condemnations of the event that come with a "but". The argument that anger against a biased media and against a society bent on subverting what they consider American values somehow justifies violence or at least places it into proper perspective, is specious. No anger can justify what happened on Wednesday.

Perhaps, (although this is factually incorrect) an election was wrongly decided. But in no rational way should this lead to ransacking the halls of government that we all supposedly hold dear. When writers in Orthodox periodicals refuse to issue a full-throated condemnation of violence and instead create a false equivalency between the ransacking of government with localized political violence this past summer, this speaks to how far our communal values have deviated. We must do serious *cheshbon hanefesh* (internal reckoning). We must be able to say unequivocally that what happened on January 6 was an onslaught on American values and Torah ideals. Without any hesitancy, we must say that it was a travesty.

Even accepting that the election was decided incorrectly (which it wasn't), *halacha* (Jewish Law) demonstrates that we should accept a single erroneous decision rather than undermine the entire governmental process. The *Sefer HaChinuch* in mitzva 496 famously explains the mitzva of *lo tassur*, understood by him to mean that we follow *Beth Din* even when they issue an erroneous ruling, articulating a social contract theory. In order to maintain society, we must accept certain risks and even errors. A system that may at times be wrong is better than no system at all. Absence of a system will allow everyone to act on his or her own wishes. This would destroy society. The *Chinuch* presents an insurmountable question to any *ben* or *bat* (male or female follower of) *Torah* who possibly felt that attempting to overturn the election was proper.

As we read *Parshas* (the weekly Torah portion of) *Shemos*, we can't fail to recognize the moral clarity of first the *meyaldos* (midwives) and then *Moshe Rabbenu* (Moses our leader). The Torah extolls those who stand against oppression in all its forms.

It is worth noting the subtle difference between the way *Moshe Rabbenu* reacted to injustice compared to the approach of the *meyaldos*. The *meyaldos* attempted to appease Pharaoh and explain away why they were unable to kill the Jewish babies. Their act of heroism was rewarded by *Hashem* (God). *Moshe Rabbenu* however develops an even clearer sense of morality. *Moshe Rabbenu* made no excuses. He could not tolerate any injustice, whether perpetrated against one of his Jewish brethren or a non-Jew. He develops from one who first was reticent to act justly (as the verse says, he turned here and there and saw there was no man) to one who acts on his sense of moral justice even when it came at great personal cost forcing him to flee *Mitzrayim* (Egypt). Moshe represents our ideal leader because he stands for pure morality and justice. The developed image of *Moshe Rabbenu* is unapologetic and unequivocal on moral matters. Like Moshe we must call out injustice. We must do so unequivocally and loudly. We must not apologize or make excuses. The attempted putsch was an unmitigated travesty and an assault on American and Torah values.

A Story's Real Heroes

Rabbi Jonathan Blake

Amid the many images from last Wednesday seared into my brain is one that inspires hope: two women in the halls of the Capitol, carrying a box full of ballots to safety, away from the rioting goons who surely would have stolen or destroyed them in their treasonous attempt to overturn the election. These two women are our Shifra and Puah, the Hebrew midwives who defied the Pharaoh's paranoid and unhinged edict to "throw the Hebrew baby boys into the Nile."

Often, a story's real heroes go unremembered, unmentioned. They put themselves at peril to do God's work without any desire for fanfare or reward. Today, we salute them and owe them a tremendous debt of gratitude.

Truth-Telling and Accountability

Rabbi Jill Zimmerman

The images of shattered glass in our nation's capital hit me in an ancestral place. *Kristallnacht*, the "night of broken glass" began the pogroms in Germany in November 1938. Synagogues and private homes were destroyed and people terrorized. This event was seeded by hatred of the "other", Jews made into the enemy and dehumanized. When you see another person as less than human, you can justify any violent action. The last five years in the United States culminated in violence and inhumanity.

I watched in horror as the glass doors to the House chamber were smashed by crazed domestic terrorists. I worried about our elected representatives on the other side. My worry was well-founded.

We wouldn't know until later about the unspeakable acts of vandalism and desecration. It was heart-breaking to see videos of barricaded doors, calls to loved ones to say goodbye in case they didn't survive this assault. To those who were fed a steady diet of "the press is an enemy of the people," smashing the press' equipment was a natural outcome. Reporters who were in the Capital building took off their press nametags, as they feared for their lives.

As always, this insanity was fueled by lies, and even worse, encouraged by those who have taken oaths to protect our democracy. Even after the looting was over, there were too many who continued to repeat the dangerous lie that the election was stolen. In the aftermath of the violence committed by mask-less people who proudly wore "Camp Aushwitz" sweatshirts and waved Confederate flags, 147 elected officials still voted against certifying the people's votes and for the racist claims that underpinned their lies.

While I understand that healing needs to take place, it needs to be grounded in both truth-telling and accountability. My own body is still reverberating with the collective trauma of broken glass. These feelings must be honored with self-compassion and patience.

Just like the Nurenburg trials after the Holocaust, we must create a plan that reveals the ugliness in broad daylight - this has to be the place where we start. People who supported the lies must be held accountable. And we must learn from this. Yes, in order to say "never again" in our nation's capital, we have to first tell the whole unvarnished truth about what led to it.

Taking a Stand
for our Democracy
Rabbi Adam Baldachin

This afternoon, I didn't recognize America. I sat, horrified at what I was watching and reading on the news about the violent insurrection on Capitol Hill in Washington, DC. I couldn't believe that this happened today in our nation's capital. I am scared, as we all are, at the security of our leaders and the future of our democracy. And I am enraged at those who wish to disenfranchise millions of people by trying to overturn a free and fair election.

At the same time, I am so proud to see our representatives back in the Capitol Building as I write this, certifying the election and fulfilling their roles to protect our democracy. Their bravery and determination to make sure that our country is not ruled by ugly mobs but by law and order is inspiring to see. It shows that our democracy is strong and able to stand up against those who try to overpower the will of the people. I am also incredibly grateful to law enforcement that secured the Capitol Building and ensured that our leaders could continue their important work.

As a Jewish American, I am very aware that America has been a great blessing for our people. We have enjoyed greater freedoms here in the past century than in any place and time outside of Israel, and our systems of government, our laws, our leaders, and the citizens that believe in this country's vision of equality are to thank for it. We can take great pride, no matter, what our political leanings, in the fact that we have recently witnessed minorities winning elections: the first black man elected to the Senate from Georgia (Rev. Dr. Raphael Warnock), the first Jew elected to the Senate from Georgia (Jon Ossoff), the first Jewish Senate

Majority Leader in US history (Chuck Schumer), and the first black woman Vice President in US history (Kamala Harris).

Let us take a few moments to check in with one another and do our part to speak up for the health of our republic. Our must raise our voices during these turbulent times in order to ensure that our treasured way of life remains possible for us and for future generations. President Abraham Lincoln once reminded Congress -- and I believe it has meaning for each of us at this moment -- "The fiery trial through which we pass, will light us down, in honor or dishonor, to the latest generation." May we gain strength from one another and our shared vision for America.

We remember Amalek so that we can erase it

Rabbi Gary S. Creditor

Two of my great-grandparents and all four of my grandparents ran away from the Amaleks of eastern Europe and came to America to find freedom - freedom from hatred, freedom from injustice, and freedom from dictatorship. When their ships neared New York City harbor, their first view was the statuesque Statue of Liberty, the lady in the harbor whose lamp was to illuminate the gate to a "promised land" that would welcome immigrants from virtually every country in the world. I wish I could have seen their faces, their smiles, their wind-blown hair and heard their hearts beat with the staccato beat that Neil Diamond captured in his song "Comin' to America." My parents, my wife, her parents, myself, our children, and grandchildren have had the privilege to be born in a singular country that promised justice and freedom from the evils of Europe that coalesced into the malevolence of Nazism and Communism. The Torah's twofold command concerning Amalek, to eradicate and remember, is embedded in the genealogical DNA of my family.

I cannot erase from my memory the consequences of Nazism. I have taught how Hitler came to power legally and used the system to convert it into a dictatorship and all the sins that then ensued. I would tell my classes, that can't happen in the United States, that we had laws, that democracy was sacrosanct, that the mob could never rule here. Despite the imperfections of this country, our motto was that we are yet perfectible, that we are a young democracy, a work in progress. When I would fly home and land in New York or Newark airports and saw "Old Glory" flying proudly, I felt safe, safer than any other place in the world. Despite the groups that hate Jews, Blacks, Latinos, Asians or any other group, the strength of our democracy made me feel safe.

For four years, my wife and I have been discussing the true reality behind Mr. Trump. It has befuddled us why no one - absolutely no one – has called him out as the twenty-first century personification of Amalek. It was evident in his every statement for more than four years, a virtual and unprecedented assault on democracy, its ideals, its values, its institutions, its visions, and its elected leadership. There was no difference between his speech on Wednesday at the Ellipse and those of the 1930's, now urging the mob to attack our secular "Holy of Holies," the heart of our democracy, our Capitol. I shudder in revulsion to even contemplate what would have been the consequences if they had succeeded. Indeed, I cry.

History is a critical instructor. We can never forget history. We can never forget Amalek. The crucial moment in the usurpation by Nazism was the burning of the Reichstag, the legislative house. Then the weak Weimar democracy was demolished. What we witnessed and endured on Wednesday was the modern incarnation of the attempt to demolish our democracy and usurp dictatorial control of the United States. We remember that the President is also commander-in-chief of the military. So was Hitler. My body shakes.

This is a threat to every single person in this country and must, through the system of law, be eliminated and its perpetrators fully punished. Amalek must be brought to justice - either while Mr. Trump is yet in office, or after January 20th. The Lady in the Harbor upon, whom countless eyes have gazed, demands that we do no less. She beckons us to stand tall, to be upright and strong for freedom, for truth, for honesty, for respect, for integrity, and for responsibility and never, ever let that light dim or be extinguished.

We remember Amalek so that we can erase it.
We remember Amalek and forget only at the danger to our democracy and at the peril of our lives.

I want my great-grandparents, grandparents, my in-laws, and my father to rest in peace in the "land of the free and the home of the brave."

The Desecration of
Our Hallowed Floor
Rabbi David-Seth Kirshner

One of the most honored and memorable moments of my professional life was when I was asked to offer a prayer in Congress. I had been to the U.S. Capitol countless times and even sat in the gallery of Congress on many occasions. But, until that day, I had never been on the hallowed floor of Congress.

I stood at the very podium where the President of the United States -- from Thomas Jefferson to today's elected leader -- stand, and offer the State of the Union. My children were given special dispensation to sit in the chamber near me while I offered the prayer, precise in its regulations and length. That dispensation was not offered to my wife or extended family who gathered to share in this moment, and instead needed to watch the proceedings from the gallery above.

After I offered the prayer, I walked exactly six paces to my right, went down three steps, and joined my daughter and son in this consecrated space as we covered our chest with our hands and recited the pledge of allegiance to the flag of our country. In that instant, I trembled with awe and cried at the holiness of the moment and the privilege I have been afforded: not only at this unique privilege, but in being granted the blessing of living in this amazing experiment, called the United States of America.

I have always been a champion of America and her rich history and order. I have proudly walked the halls of the very Capitol that is transfixed on our screens this day and lobbied elected officials for topics ranging from foreign aid to stronger gun control to equal rights for people of all sexual orientations. Each time I participated in this act, the privilege of access to our government and elected officials and the gift of living within this democracy was never lost on me. Under that great rotunda, I would regularly shudder in reverence and appreciation.

So, today, to see the chambers of the Senate being pillaged by hoodlums and thugs, to witness criminals vandalize offices of duly elected members of Congress, and to find explosive devices allegedly planted by home grown terrorists, gave me a painful feeling of violation of something that is sacred to me and, probably to you too. It hurts my eyes to watch and my soul to digest.

There was no social media or CNN when the ancient Temple was destroyed. But if there were, I envision the images that would circulate would be something akin to what we saw in today's depictions of chaos from the Capitol that will haunt me forever. Seeing ruffians in the seat of the President of the Senate snapping selfies with their feet on the dais while others vandalize and loot items from the Senate floor all while brandishing smiles was stunning and agonizing to witness. For this to happen in the place where our laws and governance emanate is equal to what the Romans did to the sanctity of Temple and, I dare -- and keenly aware -- say, what Nazis did to synagogues during World War II.

The greatest irony is these criminals are claiming that this is being done in the name of patriotism and country. Make no mistake: this is not a protest and most decidedly is not peaceful. This is terrorism.

One congregant asked me for a prayer to say in this scary moment. I was embarrassed because I could not think of prayer to say at this time. Afterall, what prayer do we utter when Capitol Police have their guns drawn and trained at those threatening to unlawfully breach the doors of the sacred halls of the Congressional chamber not to save democracy, but rather, to overthrow it? I, like you, am at a loss for prayers and words.

But we do gather. We will gather tonight, and we will say Psalms on behalf of ALL of the police, first responders and elected officials in and near Congress, many who are still in hiding, protecting our country. We will also find strength and solace in our collective (albeit virtual) gathering that has always supported us in times of crisis, worry and sadness.

In the interim, I hope you join me in praying for the safety of all in Washington DC, and to pray for the blessings and safety of these United States of America.

Where do we even start?
Rabbi Adir Glick

What do we do after witnessing the desecration of our nation? Sit back and wait for redemption and God's outstretched arm?

As we see the world falling to angry pieces. Just when you thought there was not anymore that they could throw at you.

And now, we hope the tide is turning.
But the truth is that we do not know.
We are vulnerable together.

And the upheaval and the mess is so large, nationally, internationally, between politics and pandemics.

Where do we even start?
What can we, as individuals, do?

However we each understand the story in our Parashah where God promises to deliver His people - the heavens may open. Perhaps they have already opened - But the Divine will not act single handedly to save us from our mess.

We have to play a part.

What is our role?

We find our answer in the ancient wisdom of our Rabbis in Pirkei Avot, the Ethics of the Fathers (2:11).

Lo alekha ha'melakhah ligmor, ve'lo atah ben horin le'hitbatel mi'mena

It is not incumbent upon you to complete the work, yet neither are you free to desist from it.

We must do all that we can.

We must harness the full power of our institutions, of our religious voices, of our moral, ethical, and political values, of our media - new and old - and of our commercial power as consumers and workers to make our values heard.

This is already happening in an unprecedented way.

Beyond the current crisis, as we contemplate the long healing ahead, we each have a part to play within our own spheres and environments.

To be a force of support and positivity, to be there for neighbors and friends, and family members.

To uphold each other when we feel down, and to raise our neighbor when they are struggling.

To keep our eyes open to those who have suffered the most, who cannot pay rent, are hungry, whose mental health has declined until they have lost all hope, and fallen into despair.

And to make phone calls to our elected officials.
To take part in research to help the vaccine.

To hold out our hand to those who wish to share in a prosperous and happy future and to denounce with force all those who give voice to hatred and discrimination such as Congresswoman Mary Miller of our State of Illinois who declared that "Hitler had one thing right."

At the same time, we cannot expect to complete the task. It is more than we can carry.

We need to believe that there is also a Higher Power at work in this situation.

We labor with passion and fire, and we also give up the results of all of our labor to God. This is the very definition of faith.

Right now, we do not know the meaning and significance of all that we are doing. We give it our all, but we also accept it may not go as we expect. That is ok because we do not have to carry the entire burden.

In this beautiful piece of wisdom from the Rabbis there is space for hope to be kindled.

What is hope? It is the belief that change can happen.

The Rabbis of the Mishnah knew it better than us. Their task was monumental, saving Judaism after the destruction of the Second Temple, after exile, with very few assets at their disposal. What a terrible burden they carried, but they also knew that it was not up to them to complete the task. Despite all odds, their faith played out. They did not finish.

But others came after them, who also worked, with new voices and just as much love and devotion to the cause. It never did achieve the perfect result because that is not the nature of the world itself. But the work continues on.

As we discovered in last week's parashah Shemot, God revealed His name to Moses as *"Eheyeh Asher Eheyeh,"* literally *"I will be that I will be."* The Hassidic master Rebbe Levi Yitzchak says that those words mean *"I am always more than what you are able to imagine. You cannot put Me into a box."*

We never achieve perfection. The task is never completed, because life is ever changing. The Divine is always unfolding.

We get short periods of rest from our labors. But then the wheel starts to spin again - we would not have it any other way. It would go against our nature and the nature of the world.

Although we have been using the word 'unprecedented' a lot over the past months, the truth is that every generation uses it. Because every generation faces monumental challenges. People are always both more foolish and more wise than we remember.

When it is bad, we cry.
And when it is good, we forget.

It is why the midrash says, King Solomon had written on his ring, gam zeh ya'avor, this too shall pass. To remember when times are bad - this too shall pass. And to remember when times are good - this too shall pass.

When we despair and cannot see how we can fulfill the task ahead, we need to remember the lesson of our parashah, that the seemingly impossible can occur.

As David ben Gurion said, "In order to be a realist, you must believe in miracles." We too have experienced miracles, big and small, as individuals and as a people.

I remember when my parents told me of how they danced in the street with joy after the miraculous Entebbe operation to rescue the hostages, at a time after the Yom Kippur War when the situation looked very dark.

If there is any teaching from this parashah, it is that miracles do occur; to heal the deepest wounds, to shake the powerful, to bring the destitute and powerless home.

It may not always manifest as we hope. But we have to remain faith-filled and hope-filled, and remember that it is a partnership. It is not upon me to complete the task nor am I free to desist from it.

In the space of that hope, we can be empowered vessels for the forces of the universe. We can accomplish greater missions and fulfill grand dreams.
We can shake the world.

But we cannot do it alone.
We need each other and we need the power of Spirit.

Ribbono Shel Olam, O Master of the Universe
Don't let us lose hope.
Don't let us forget that we each have a role.
Give us strength to keep on trying.
Help us to complete the task.
Heal our broken nation and world.

On Grief and Grounds for Hope

Rabbi Jen Gubitz

Shoulders slightly hunched, a blue pen in hand, he wears a gray windowpane suit. He stands at the lectern and a black mask covers his face. Looking down to read his notes: "We are not here, Madam Speaker, to vote for the candidate we want," he says, "we are here to recognize the candidate the people actually voted for." News reports shared that "House lawmakers in both parties stood and delivered a rousing ovation." These words, like many we heard on Wednesday, were powerful.

But it's not the words so much as it is the image. For when you look closer, on the lapel of his suit is a congressional pin and below it a shiva ribbon ripped with grief. Because on Tuesday, Representative Jamie Raskin stood at his son's graveside. And on Wednesday, he showed up to the house chambers to certify the electoral college vote. This image tears at my heart —that Representative Raskin mourns his brilliant son whos truggled with the "blindingly painful and merciless 'disease called depression.'"

And it tears at my heart that Raskin — who should have been sitting in his shiva house is instead standing on the floor of the House chambers in a grey windowpane suit. What a window into the pain and grief of it all.

"Mommy, why is that man breaking a window?" she asks. Nola Bea, my niece, turned 7 last week. My brother's eldest, she is truly the first beloved of the next generation of Gubitzim.

She is wise and thoughtful, very silly and very observant.

"Dominate the day," my brother tells her each morning as she heads off to school. "Be curious, be kind," my sister-in-law lovingly reminds. But Nola Bea was home from school on Wednesday watching a man breaking a window because schools in New Orleans have returned to remote learning because the virus is…well, the virus…This story breaks my heart.

Nola Bea should have been at school being kind, being curious, dominating the day. Except the virus and all the mismanagement… She should've been at school, not at home asking her mommy "Why is that that man breaking a window?"

And while a fair question on a normal day, Wednesday was not a normal day. Rather, Wednesday was a window into the many chambered heart of our country.

Grief and disbelief. How could this be? And what is at the heart of it all? And so I vacillate between these two images and so many others that have crossed our screens these past days, weeks, months, years.

My jaw drops. Is this real?

Having walked those corridors of congress so many times as a RAC Legislative Assistant, then as a rabbi with teens raising their voices on Capitol Hill, whether in Lugar or Warren's offices, amid multiple administrations and the spectrum of politics, it was always respectful even when we disagreed. What is at the heart of it all? How could this be?

And so I vacillate among what we now call the cycles of grief, for it is not linear and never complete, back and forth between the two images: of a lawmaker setting aside even the greatest of family priority —grieving his son — in order to carry out his commitment to our country, and the child asking: "Why is it this way, mom?"

And why is it this way that the response of the summer's fight for justice for the lives of black and brown and indigenous people, why was that response met with troops and guns and armor?

And why was the response of this week from white supremacist insurrection more or less met with a loving escort from the building as if to say — "come again soon" after looting Lady Freedom's chambers?

For those who have memories nearer or further than my own, do you also vacillate between them, asking how could this be? Or asserting, No! These are not the ways of the world!

Then what are the ways of the world?
What is at the heart of it all?
And, do we have any grounds for hope?

At the heart of it all is, of course, our Torah.

This Shabbat we begin a new book, a new chapter — *Shemot*, Exodus. Within it are so many images that frame the history and memory of the Jewish people.

It is hard to believe all that occurs in just one Torah portion: From a new pharaoh who knew not Joseph forbidding Israelites to birth baby boys to Egyptian midwives Shifra and Puah defying orders from Pharoah continuing to help Israelite women deliver their children.

One such child, Moses, is born, placed in the Nile, then brought forth from the Nile by the daughter of Pharaoh, he is raised in the palace.

He sees injustice for the first time, notices the plight of his Israelite people, and acts on it violently. He runs away to

Midian where he meets Tzippora. Out tending the flocks, he comes across a bush that is burning yet not consumed. He encounters God who also hears the plight of the people. And Moses, a reluctant prophet, begins to understand the signs and wonders of God's power and of his own voice within. And then joined by Aaron, he goes to Pharaoh to redeem his people.

Wow! What a Torah portion! And what good timing for us to glue ourselves to this narrative instead of the news, giving us grounds for hope.

You see, while sometimes there are leaders who knew not Joseph, there are other leaders who did and do, and who know from goodness and mercy.

And sometimes, as we have seen, there are leaders who have finally stated (albeit too late) that we will not tolerate a heartless tyrant like Pharaoh, that we will not let our home become as if biblical Egypt. And there are people who despite not knowing the ways the health of our world will endure are still delivering children into this world, each one a Moses, a Miriam, a Tommy Raskin, a Nola Bea Gubitz.

And each supported by Shifras and Puahs midwives, medical professionals, essential service workers shepherding us into as much safety as their own hands will allow.

Not to mention those, whether elected officials casting votes or those Puahs and Shifras,
whose name shares the root with shofar
as if calling out, and calling up,
phone bank-by-phone bank,
post card-by-post card,
fighting voter suppression and reclaiming our vote,
midwifing us,
Stacey Abrams-ing us,
Rebecca DeHart-ing us,

John Lewis-ing us.
delivering us
into a world of justice and equity

such that a Black, Indian American, female Vice President and a Catholic President could restore dignity to our highest office, and a Black preacher and a Jewish man could walk the halls of congress hand in hand.

I can keep going...

The Torah is just that wise... and these are our grounds for hope. As we know, the Exodus journey is a long one. It eventually leads us to our own Seder tables recounting the joy and the sorrow, the plagues and the freedom, the cries and the songs of the Jewish people. And then we wander for a long time in a desert. But let us revel for a moment longer on these grounds for hope.

For when Moses encounters a bush that is burning yet not consumed: "I must turn aside," he says, "to look at this marvelous sight; "Why," he wonders, "why doesn't the bush burn up?" (Exodus 3:3).

Shifting his perspective, he wonders: "How could this be so?" As if to say, can there, in fact, be fire that does *NOT* burn everything down? God calls to Moses and "*Hineni*, Here I am," Moses responds.
"Do not come closer," says God.
"Remove your sandals from your feet, take off your shoes, for the place on which you stand is holy ground (Exodus 3:5).

Y'all, I don't know about you, but I haven't worn shoes in weeks. I'm not even wearing them now. This call must be for us! Offering us the grounds for hope!

There will certainly be
more pain, more virus,
more racism, more hatred,
but lest we allow the part of Wednesday's horrific events -
and they were horrific - lest we permit them to drown out
the watershed moments
of what happens when collective power
pursuing a more just world,
led by black women no less,
rises up and wins.

Don't forget to ride that wave a little longer.
So we will continue to hold it all,
this breadth of human experience.
From Congressman Raskin's grief,
to Nola Bea's questions,
to the visionary leadership of the Shifras and Puahs
and Miriams and Yocheveds
and Tzipporas and Bat Pharoahs,
and to Moses's transformational journey
to lead the people — *us* — to freedom.

And we hold our grief while standing firmly on these
grounds for hope.

So, as my family says, in these days and weeks to come,
let us be curious, let us be kind, and let us dominate these
days together.

Our nation's holy space was sullied today

Rabbi Eytan Hammerman

וַיֹּאמֶר אַל־תִּקְרַב הֲלֹם שַׁל־נְעָלֶ֫יךָ מֵעַל רַגְלֶ֫יךָ כִּי הַמָּקוֹם אֲשֶׁר אַתָּה עוֹמֵד עָלָיו
אַדְמַת־קֹדֶשׁ הוּא:

And God said, "Do not come closer. Remove your
sandals from your feet, for the place on which you stand
is holy ground (Exodus 3:5)

With these words, to be read this coming Shabbat morning
as we begin the Book of Exodus, God instructs Moses to
approach the Burning Bush and reveals God-self to Moses.
Their unparalleled relationship begins at that hallowed site
in the desert.

Hallowed, holy grounds are, at times, places of religious
gathering - synagogues, churches, mosque and temples. My
breath was taken away two years ago when I first came
upon Vatican Square; I had the same experience fifteen
summers back at the Temples of Angkor Wat, Cambodia.
Many of us feel this way when we see the Kotel/Western
Wall, especially for the first time. These religious sites are
sacred ground, not only to their particular religious
adherents. Sometimes, we have similar reactions when we
visit places of great natural beauty; many among us consider
places like the Grand Canyon or even a beach at sunset to
have elevated spiritual status. And places of civic import are
hallowed as well.

Six years ago, I was given one of the greatest honors an
American clergyperson can receive, an invitation to offer the
Opening Prayer in the United States House of
Representatives. Congressman Sean Patrick Maloney,
whose district includes Mahopac, NY, nominated me as

"Guest Chaplain" of the House in June, 2014, a day that I will surely always consider among the most sacred of my life. Standing at the rostrum of the House, I felt a sense of spirituality similar to what I feel presiding over a Neilah service to conclude Yom Kippur. I felt a perception of sacredness on par with what I feel standing beside a couple under a Chuppah. I experienced a level of elevated holiness akin to when I am called to bless a Bar or Bat Mitzvah. It was a personal religious experience of the highest level to stand and, even in just one hundred words, to deliver hope and prayer to the assembled Members of Congress (and all who watched on C-SPAN).

Yesterday's actions inside the U.S. Capitol were acts of national and religious desecration. The scenes from Washington should remind us of synagogues being ransacked and cemeteries defiled. Our nation's holy space was sullied today, a dark day in a dark period for our country. As Jews, we know what it means to have our holiest places soiled. That is what occurred today, on Capitol Hill.

The Conservative Movement's organizations reminded us this week that the basis for our democracy stems from the Torah's belief that every person is created equally in God's image and is therefore entitled to equal representation in government and equal protection under the law. Each week we pray during our Shabbat worship to "uproot from our hearts hatred and malice, jealousy and strife. Plant love and companionship, peace and friendship, among the many people and faiths who dwell in our nation."

The statement concluded:

> "This prayer is more than an expression of faith. It is a call to action, and we have much work to do to heal the deep wounds and divisions which afflict our beloved country and society. May our new leaders, who are coming to power this month at every level of

government, rise to the responsibility the voters have entrusted to them, to bring healing and exercise responsible governance."

Amen!!

Silence is an
Act of Agreement
Rabbi Eli Garfinkel

The Book of Exodus begins with a transformation. Like a butterfly emerging from a chrysalis, the tribal clan known as the sons of Jacob becomes a nation, the Children of Israel.

The Children of Israel appear in verse 7 of chapter 1. Antisemitism, the hatred of the Jewish people, appear in verse 9 of chapter 1. We exist as a nation for just two verses, and then the hatred of our people blooms like mold on bread.

The first person to express an antisemitic thought is Pharaoh himself. In verses 9 and 10, he says, "And he said to his people, 'Look, the Israelite people are much too numerous for us. Let us deal shrewdly with them, so that they may not increase; otherwise in the event of war they may join our enemies in fighting against us and rise from the ground.'"

Why did Pharaoh fear that the Children of Israel would rise from the ground, *Alah min Haaretz*? Normally, we would think that means "they will leave the country," they will *alah*, make aliyah to Israel.

But that doesn't make sense because Pharaoh was complaining that there were too many Israelites in Egypt. He should *want* them to leave Egypt, so the words "rise from the ground" must mean something else.

Rabbi Yaakov Tzvi Mecklenburg, better known by the name of his book, *HaKtav V'HaKabbalah*, suggests another way to understand the verse. He says that when Pharaoh expressed fear that the Israelites would rise from the ground, he meant that they would become the leaders of Egypt, that they would end up running the show.

This makes sense to me, and it is classic antisemitism. Pharaoh was the first person to look at a Jew and say, "Those people are going to start bossing us around."

Pharaoh's evil opinion turns into evil action in verse 11, when the King of Egypt enslaves the people and forces them to toil in the fields. His plan backfires, as the Torah notes in verse 12: "But the more they were oppressed, the more they increased and spread out, so that the [Egyptians] came to dread the Israelites."

It only takes a grand total of six verses for Pharaoh's hatred to turn into enslavement and then into genocide. In verse 16, he tells the midwives to kill all the newborn baby boys.

This is the natural course of antisemitism. It starts with worrying about our power, then that worry turns into fear, that fear becomes injustice, and then it's just a hop, skip, and a jump from there to the Crusades, the Inquisition, the slaughters committed by Chmielnicki, and the death camps of the 20th century.

Even though we live in America, Jews must be on constant watch for antisemitism. The lesson of the Holocaust is that we cannot assume that any country will forever remain kind to us. So long as we insist on existing, there will be those who insist on our annihilation, that's simply the way of the world, as the Sages say: *Eisav Sonei Et Yaakov*, Esau hates Jacob.

Some have asked me why I made my public statement condemning the President for what happened on Wednesday at the Capitol. Am I saying that all or even most Republicans and conservatives are guilty? Of course not. My disappointment and anger is aimed only at the President himself, not at any movement or philosophy.

I am not criticizing 75 million people. I don't have that right. I'm criticizing one person. What scared me about Wednesday was that the President allowed, or encouraged, or simply stood by while an antisemitic mob to commit horrendous acts of vandalism and violence that led to at least two deaths.

That is what I find shocking and unforgivable. If he was opposed to what happened, then he should have put down Twitter and gone out there with a bullhorn and demanded a stop to the riot.

But the President, so desperate for support and so thirsty for approval, will accept it from anybody, even terrible people like the antisemites who have infected his ranks of support. We first saw this at Charlottesville and now again on Capitol Hill.

Let me tell you about the disgusting antisemitism that was witnessed and documented at the riot on Wednesday. There was at least one man wearing a shirt that said 'Camp Auschwitz' on the front and 'Staff' on the back.

Let me say that again so it sinks in: There was at least one man wearing a shirt that said 'Camp Auschwitz' on the front and 'Staff' on the back. And there was another who wore a shirt that said "Work makes you free," the English translation of *Arbeit Macht Frei*, the very words that greeted new arrivals at Auschwitz's gate.

There were swastikas and references to ZOG, what their ilk calls the Zionist Occupied Government. There were placards and shirts emblazoned with the slogan "6MWE," which is short for "Six Million Wasn't Enough." There were other signs that expressed doubt that the Holocaust ever happened. And there was the usual cabal of weirdos who hate the Jews because we practice *b'rit milah.*

Were all of the rioters antisemites? No. In fact, some of the rioters were Orthodox Jews, one of them the son of a prominent judge. His brother claims that he was pushed inside the Capitol and never intended to enter.

You'll pardon my skepticism. That kind of sounds like Aaron in the Torah who said to Moses, "This golden calf just walked out of the fire."

We must not make the mistake of thinking that the presence of some Jews there makes the event kosher. It means that some Jews there did not understand the nature of the event they had joined. They didn't comprehend that they had entered the belly of the beast with some very bad and dangerous people.

In addition to the antisemites and Holocaust deniers, there were racists of other kinds as well, and we can safely assume that white supremacists do not like the Jews, either. There were conspiracy theorists, too, with their crazy ideas that fly in the face of reality.

For instance, there was a heavy presence of Qanon followers, and Qanon is also in bed with antisemitism, as it believes that a group of cosmopolitan globalists secretly runs the world. That is all obvious coded language for Jews, and members of Qanon have spread their hatred all of the internet.

Combine all this with the vandalism, and the bombs, and the zip ties, and the nooses, and you have the makings of a frightful disaster. I honestly felt and still do feel that I had no choice but to condemn what had happened in public. It was a moment when I said, "I have to sleep at night, I have to look at myself in the mirror."

I typically enjoy being neutral about political topics. I used to love talking about politics back in the 80s when you could express an unpopular opinion without fear. Nowadays, it's rarely worth the bother. Having said that, there are times when silence is very loud, and had I been silent about Wednesday, it would have been an act of agreement. I cannot agree with or tolerate what happened.

Yes, I know that the Black Lives Matter protestors also rioted violently, and I looked it up — at the time I said in a sermon that those riots should have been put down by force if necessary. Yes, I know that those riots also included some antisemites and that a couple of synagogues were spray-painted. As that old song puts it, the freaks come out at night. But what happened at the Capitol is a different beast entirely, one that is more dangerous and threatening.

The BLM riots reminded me of the LA riots of the 90s. They may have reminded some of you of the Newark riots of the 1960s. Wednesday's riot reminded me of *Kristallnacht*.

This country needs healing, and the wounds we have cannot be solved with political change. The inauguration of a new president, as welcome as it might be for some, will not help. Our issues are moral and spiritual; they go to the core of who we are as people.

Let us pray that there will be no more violence and that Americans will learn to embrace the people with whom they disagree. Let us also pray that those who hate the Jews will repent of their evil ways and come back to the human race.

After the Capitol Hill Insurrection

Rabbi Joseph B. Meszler

Last Tuesday night, before Wednesday's events, the topic we happened to discuss in our Confirmation class was on free speech, hate speech, and incitement. We talked about *sinat chinam* - senseless hatred. Also, at about this time last year we had our annual Confirmation trip to Washington DC. When images of the mob were posted inside the Capitol, I recognized some of those places, and I imagine some of our students did as well.

Also during last year's Confirmation DC trip, some of our students got a lesson when we ran into a demonstration against then-candidate Michael Bloomberg's office by a similar kind of crowd, and the signs spelled Bloomberg's name with the O's being swastikas and the hammer and sickle.

It is tempting to give my version of an op-ed, but you don't need that. I will say, in the spirit of the Hebrew prophets, that we need to call out incitement, racism, antisemitism, and incredible hypocrisy. You don't get to condemn the fire when you helped pour the gasoline.

Rioting of any kind should not be glamorized. Nor should we indulge in "whataboutism" and draw false equivalencies. But certainly, what happened on Wednesday was a uniquely dark day. It was also completely foreseeable and preventable, and that is on us.

We are a deeply divided nation, but we are not caught in an inevitable spiral of fate. This week can be a wake-up call and choice to never repeat this past period of time. We can personally take responsibility for our democracy. It is not enough to pay our taxes, serve on a jury, and occasionally vote. We need to be actively involved in creating the society we want to be a part of.

In this week's Torah portion, we read about Moses at the burning bush. Moses sees a bush on fire, but it is not consumed. Our nation, too, can sometimes be aflame, but we will not be consumed, not if we take care of our home.

In this spirit, I have written a Prayer for the United States, to be read responsively. The responses are all verses from the Hebrew Bible or quotations from the Talmud. I hope you see this as a return to our most basic values.

Prayer for the United States

Let us, we the people of the United States, return to our sacred principles.
> *Practice justice, truth and peace in your gates.*
> (Zechariah 8:16)

Let us engage in dialogue with civility and decency, striving together for the common good.
> *Every argument that is for the sake of heaven shall endure, and every argument not for the sake of heaven shall not endure.* (Avot 5:27)

Let us be ready to sacrifice for our country and appreciate and honor those who keep us secure, who uphold our laws, and who save our lives.
> *Be strong and have courage.* (Deuteronomy 31:6)

Let us respect each other, defend the dignity of young and old, and protect the vulnerable.

God created humanity in the divine image. Love your neighbor as yourself (Genesis 1:27, Leviticus 19:19)

Let us discern how we contribute to the problems of our land, and let us atone for our nation's sins.
> *Turn us back to you, O God, and we shall return. Renew our days as a new beginning.*
> (Lamentations 5:21)

Let us hold each other accountable.
> *Learn to do good; seek justice, and correct oppression.*
> (Isaiah 1:17)

God, protect us against arrogance, ignorance, bigotry, greed, violence, and lies.
> *Lying speech is an abomination to the Eternal, but those who act faithfully are pleasing to God.* (Proverbs 12:22)

Let us safeguard the lives, freedoms, and opportunities of each one of us of every race, religion, and identity.
> *Proclaim liberty throughout the land to all its inhabitants.* (Leviticus 25:10)

Let us pursue just ends with just means.
> *Justice, justice shall you pursue.* (Deuteronomy 16:18)

Let us strengthen our democracy and defend it.
> *For the work of righteousness shall be peace, and the effect of righteousness, calm and confidence forever.*
> (Isaiah 32:17)

Let us learn from and teach one another, celebrating uniqueness, diversity and unity.
> *Praised are You, Eternal our God, Ruler of the universe, who makes each one of Your creations different.*
> (Berakhot 58b)

May we now renew our faith in our country and take responsibility for its future.

Everyone will sit under their own vine and fig tree, and no one will make them afraid. (Micah 4:4)

And let us say together:
Amen.

When to Weep and When to Laugh

Rabbi David-Seth Kirshner

I want to share a story from the Talmud (*Masechet Makkot*) that has been swirling about in my mind for the past 36 hours. The story is below, and I used some editorial license in my translations.

> It once was that Rabban Gamliel, Rabbi Elazar ben Azarya, Rabbi Yehoshua, and Rabbi Akiva were walking towards Jerusalem soon after the destruction of the Temple. When they arrived at Mount Scopus and saw (which you can still see clearly today from that peak) the site of where the Temple once stood, they tore their garments, in keeping with religious practices of mourning. They then went down to the scene of the destruction. When they arrived at the Temple Mount, they saw a fox that emerged from the site of what was once the Holy of Holies, (which was tantamount to us today, seeing rats infest this space that used to be sanctified and holy). The Rabbis all began weeping among the ruins, and Rabbi Akiva was laughing. The rabbis asked Akiva: "For what reason are you laughing?" Rabbi Akiva said to them: "For what reason are you weeping?"

> They replied to him: "We are weeping because this is the place concerning which it is written: 'And the non-priest who approaches shall die' (and now foxes walk in it; and shall we not weep? They meant that this used to be our holy place and now it is in ruins and infested with unseemly animals).

> They said to Rabbi Akiva: "For what reason are you laughing?" Rabbi Akiva retorted to them: "I am laughing, as it is written when God revealed the future to the

75

prophet Isaiah: 'And I will take to Me faithful witnesses to attest: Uriah the priest, and Zechariah the son of Jeberechiah.'"

Akiva was laughing because he felt that this moment of sadness and destruction brought each person closer to redemption and unity and an opportunity to rebuild the Temple and have Jewish unity.

In the wake of the unspeakable siege on the Capitol and appalling assault on our democracy, I am not sure if I should weep or laugh. I am puzzled as to whether this is the end of a terrible period and the beginning of something great or the end of something great and the beginning of something terrible.

When stewing over the recent events and pondering over this ancient story, I have come to realize that if we are to laugh or cry, to be like Rabbi Azaryah or Rabbi Akiva, is ultimately up to us to not only decide but to shape the reality we hope for. The world we want to live within is far more than something we wish or yearn for. It is something we shape with our words, our hands, our actions, and our hearts. Change does not happen through hope. It starts with hope and then is materialized with our energy and actions and work.

I have decided that I want to laugh, like Rabbi Akiva, and believe that our best days are in front of us. I want this to be a moment of national unity and collective resolve. The future I want to see come to fruition is one of possibility, peace, love, tolerance, and compassion. Today, I will begin the hard work of turning those hopes into reality. With my hand outstretched and wide open towards you, join me in this sacred journey. The work begins now.

Do you remember?

Jennifer Rudick Zunikoff

Do you remember when

pandemics and vigilantes and
attacking capitol buildings and
building a gallows with
a swinging noose and
wearing your Jew hate on your chest

Lived long ago and far away?

It lives right-this-minute and in-your-face
It is spitting acid in your eyes

Who Are We?
Rabbi Noah Farkas

As the events unfolded yesterday on Capitol Hill, I like so many, was taken aback by the brazen and swift insurrection by domestic terrorists. Four people died, dozens of peace officers were wounded, the Confederate Flag, a symbol of hatred and racism, was paraded through statuary hall for the first time in U.S. history. It was shameful and embarrassing as a nation to see what has been a platform for stability in the world, the U.S. Government, become so exposed so quickly.

While the riot lasted only a short time, it is enough to ask abiding questions about our democracy, our values and the very fabric of our country. At one point, I posted about how embarrassed I was, saying "we are better than this," and I was surprised by the pushback I received questioning whether America, and people in general, are better than being a mob. Critics quickly pointed out that one can draw a "straight line from the [Compromise of 1877], (ending the Reconstruction era) to the riot." Others took a more existential view, sending memes and questioning whether or not people are capable of anything like progress. Curiously, many of the interlocutors of my post are some of the most progressive people I know.

This bewildering moment in history is a reckoning. There is no question of that, but what is it a reckoning of, exactly? Is it political, social or communal? It's hard to say in the ever nebulous haze of the present tense, but to me the question all of us must deal with is deeper. It is an inner question. It is a spiritual question:

Who are we really? Is there more the human spirit than vicious animus, or are we made of more sacred stuff?

I find it cynical to simply agree with the prejudice that modern science tells us about our conception of the self. Many neuroscientists say that the self can be reduced to the hundred million or so wisps of pulp firing off inside our heads. Our mental life, comprising our thoughts, ambitions, passions, our love, our fear - everything that we think of as our most intimate selves - is the activity of these little specks of jelly.

Life, the philosopher Martin Buber writes, "is more than the sum of goal-directed verbs." The entirety of ourselves is not found in the manipulation of things, people, or even experiences. The "I" in each of us, is something that lives in the world and through it, in relation to something much greater than each of ourselves. We are, as the writer David Foster Wallace writes, "both flesh and not." And iIf there is anything that runs through our tradition as Jews, it's that progress is possible. Tomorrow does not have to look like yesterday. Liberation is possible. Goodness is sovereign, even if clouded or eclipsed by particular moments of chaos.

The rabbis say that when God revealed God's self to the masses, God appeared as a mirror, reflecting the myriad of Israelites in the light of revelation. (Pesikta D'Rav Kahana 12:22) In God's mirror, we find the answer to our own deepest questions. Never before has a culture said that your tomorrows do not have to look like your yesterdays. Never before has a book said that the part of you that feels unworthy, enslaved, downtrodden, and disempowered, shall have eternal sovereignty.

Judaism's answer to the question of ourselves is to look in God's mirror, and see that we live for a future that while unseen, can be created. To reflect the Divine image is to know that we are the sacred capacity to imagine a world, to repent for our misgivings, to repair the breach, to forgive trespass, and to liberate the soul. It is the life we lead towards greatness. God's name in Exodus is ours and ours is God's. We will be what we will ourselves to be.

At this moment in history, we cannot answer the question "Who are we?" with only the smallest, most narrow of answers. We are better than our darkest proclivities. If we make the turn towards the future, if we choose to see the light, if we look into God's mirror, we can grow, we can change, we can speak with kings, we can claim our place. When we extend ourselves beyond our limits and partner with what is holy, we can tell the most important story of all - the story of goodness.

I wish we could take the whole country to the mikvah

Rabbi Ilan Glazer

I can't help but think that today's violence and thuggery in DC is a symptom of a larger addiction gripping too many in the US and around the world: the disease of toxic individuality and me-first-ism, the disease of intolerance and the addiction to victimhood, and they're-out-to-get-me-itis. Of course, racism is a large part of what feeds the right-wing beast, and anti-Semitism also rears its ugly head too often.

I wanted Trump to be a leader who would work for the common good, but I didn't honestly think he had it in him. Seemed pretty clear to so many of us years ago that he was incompetent and deceitful, and interested in his own ego and power first. Is it any surprise that after four years listening to his hateful brew that people would act on what he tells them?

Johann Hari says the opposite of addiction is connection. We need to reconnect with people who don't look like us, act like us, or live in the same media bubbles as us. We need to remember that everyone living on this planet is created in God's image, and that, as Reb Zalman said, *"the only way to get it together is together."* Someone else said: *"an enemy is simply someone who's story you haven't yet heard."*

To be fair, I think everyone who participated in today's violence should be arrested and face the consequences, along with everyone who encouraged the violence to happen. And then they should have mandatory sessions where they are forced to hear the stories of others who don't share their views. I am all in favor of positive brainwashing.

We can hold onto our narrow stories of who we think we are, or we can break out of our self-imposed identities and grow. I understand that for so many, protesting and committing violence is seen as a solution to the odds feeling stacked against them. And I wish they understood the narcissism, privilege, and toxic beliefs that contribute to their understanding and actions.

January 20th will arrive, and I hope the next administration can help heal this country. Lord knows we need it. I wish we could take the whole country to the mikvah and start over.

Alas, we will just have to roll up our sleeves and participate in the hard work of making America the country it's meant to be. I pray that we have the courage and wisdom to do so.

A Glimmer of Hope

Rabbi Rachel Ain

Friends, we have all been reflecting on the events of this week that took place in our nation's capital.

Our country was rocked as we witnessed scenes of the Confederate flags in the Capitol, individuals with "Camp Auschwitz" and "6MWE" (6 Million Weren't Enough) t-shirts. The sacred halls of Congress were ransacked forcing our elected officials under their desks. These were painful images for all of us. Leaders who incited and displayed sympathy for these rioters was not only unacceptable, but dangerous. Words matter and we cannot excuse speech that seeks to undermine our democracy. Many political commentators and other experts will have much to weigh in on regarding the impact of this week on America, but we are reminded that Judaism teaches that words have the power to create worlds and words have the power to destroy worlds.

I have been trying to find the proper response to the events of this week and I am honored to be on the executive committee of the NY Board of Rabbis who, in partnership with many other faith leaders, penned the following statement:

> Our respective faith traditions require that we make moral distinctions in our lives between the permitted and the prohibited. We distinguish between civil discourse and malicious denigration, peaceful protest and insurrection. We cannot be silent when we hear and see those who willingly violate the core values of our democracy. As faith leaders, we expound from our pulpits and our communities that words have consequences. We understand the responsibility of preaching truth, justice and lovingkindness. What we say

with our mouths may influence what others do with their hands.

We expect that our President and those in positions of leadership to create the common ground upon which we can respectfully disagree with one another without demonizing an opponent as the enemy. The bronze Statue of Freedom crowns the Capitol Building in Washington, D.C. as a beacon of hope and union for all Americans. Freedom of speech does not permit or condone incitement or insurgency. The storming of the United States Capitol is unjustifiable and those who perpetrated this violence must be lawfully punished.

We commend our Congressional leaders who in a bipartisan decision reconvened following the desecration and dangerous display of violence to certify the electoral results. They demonstrated to the world that our democracy will not be deterred by anyone seeking its destruction.

We pray that President-elect Biden and Vice President-elect Harris will lead our country with decency and dignity so that we may continue to live in a democracy not a mob-ocracy, with room for all to respect one another.

These voices of religious leaders from across the religious and political spectrum offer a glimmer of hope. At a moment when our country feels broken, we must use our words as they are intended, to create, not to destroy, to build up, not to tear down, and we must look for moments of light, seeping through the darkness, to remind us that though weeping may tarry for the night, joy will come in the morning.

Our Country Needs Us

Rabbi Morris Zimbalist

Posted on Facebook and emailed to the members of Congregation Beth Judea in Long Grove, IL.

Words matter, but oftentimes silence speaks louder than words.

I denounce the shameful, disgraceful, disgusting, despicable, and reckless actions of the protesters at the Capitol!! The lack of leadership from the highest levels of government is appalling. Where is the "one nation, under God, indivisible?" Democracy is being attacked, not by foreign countries despising the values of freedom and democracy, but by Americans driven by chaos, disorder, and radical dissension. This is a painful reminder that America must have leaders of goodwill who see way beyond themselves.

Republicans and Democrats, all races and religions, people of all abilities and orientations, and all who believe in peace and humanity, it is time to begin the process of healing. The time is long overdue. Each of us needs to lead and model for others the virtues which have historically defined America: life, liberty, the pursuit of happiness, justice, equality, law and order, and the list goes on.

May God bless America and give our nation strength during this unfathomable time to restore the beacon of light that our country represents for its people and the world that has been dimmed by the shadows of fear, incitement, and violence.

I want to recognize that there are a lot of emotions filling each of us. I know among those emotions are feelings of frustration, anger, dismay, disgust, hopelessness, and the list goes on. I'm very sorry that so many of us are upset and concerned. I am too.

In the Book of Ecclesiastes we learn (1:4)

> *"Dor Holeich, v'dor bah, v'ha'aretz li'olam omedet – One generation goes, and another generation comes, and the world stands firm forever."*

This teaching speaks to the importance of memory – the knowledge that there is a cycle to life – and that the result of transition and change must be communal stability. We are reminded about how quickly stability, society, and governance can change in the opening words of this week's Torah portion – *Parashat Shemot*. Just after naming the generations of Jacob who journeyed down to Egypt, and immediately following the death of Joseph – arguably one of the most outspoken leaders in the Torah who could speak to the interests of both the Israelites and Egyptians – the Torah states (1:8),

> *"Va'yakom Melech chadash al Mitzrayim asher lo yadah et Yosef – A new king arose in Egypt who did not know Yosef."*

In other words, the greater governance of the Egyptians did not see the need for diplomacy. The Egyptians falsely concluded and truly believed that they were better than all the others.

They were right and the Israelites were wrong. And through fear, intimidation, violence, and an inability to recognize and respect the differences among people a brutal period of time in the history of the Jewish people began. We remind ourselves of it every year, and at our Passover seders we thank God for taking us from slavery to freedom, from grief to joy, from mourning to festivity, from darkness to light, and ultimately to redemption. Not a single man or a single woman did that amazing feat by themselves. God did it. And through faith and communal desire the Israelites united in a sacred purpose to experience a better, brighter, and more peaceful future. The road ahead was not easy. Moses, Aaron, Miriam, and Joshua were very different people and none of them were flawless leaders with a perfect system of governance for the greater people. This style of leadership and governance has remained consistent throughout all time and continues to this day.

It is the reality that we live with every day: No person is perfect. No government lacks flaws. People have different ideas and opinions. People believe they are right while others are wrong. People can agree and people can disagree. But civility and respect are among the needed components for these complicated relationships and systems to work. They are requirements to create a peaceful and prosperous world for all people.

The Preamble of the United States Constitution reads,

> *"We the people of the United States, in order to form a more perfect Union, establish justice, ensure domestic tranquility, provide for the common defense, promote the general welfare, and secure the blessings of liberty to ourselves and our posterity, do ordain and establish this Constitution for the United States of America."*

Our Preamble reminds us that our nation is not perfect and that we are a work in progress. The goals within this process include justice, peace, safety, and freedom to live our lives surrounded by the blessings of health, happiness, and prosperity.

The events that took place at the United States Capitol yesterday were disgraceful. They remind us that democracy is fragile and imperfect. As a political observer, I fear that the two major political parties in our country that so many of us identify with and hold dear are too often becoming "absolutists" in their views and ideologies – in other words, one Party must always be right and the other Party must always be wrong. It is black or white and the space in between lacks any shade of gray. Extreme ideologies are often marginalized by fellow members of their Party of choice as well as by members of the opposing Party. But I fear these extremist views and ideologies are bleeding into mainstream political thought. The tone of disagreements increasingly lack civility. Respect for differing views has diminished. And the lack of desire to live peacefully with our differences, faults, and imperfections continues to plague our country and the greater world.

Tonight, though, we need to focus on the violence that infiltrated our nation's Capitol Building – the epicenter of American democracy and the sanctuary for all members of Congress to discuss and debate the best interests of our country and the American people. We have a right for peaceful protests and have executed that right throughout history. Peaceful protests can lead to productive change. But when protests become riots the aftermath is riddled with death and destruction. We have seen this too frequently in our country from organizations identifying both as liberals and as conservatives. I am truly sorry that this destructive behavior and lethal actions exist in our country. I apologize for not condemning more of those behaviors more publicly. All people responsible for the lawlessness in our country need to be held accountable. The attack on the Capitol, though, was an attack on each and every one of us and values that we strive for as Americans. Broken windows can be fixed. Broken chairs, desks, and name plates can be replaced. Broken trust, broken hearts, and broken spirits take much longer to repair and risk remaining damaged or broken forever.

That is exactly why we must come together as the American people. The violence at the Capitol is the antithesis of who we are. As peace-loving people, I believe that we not only have a responsibility to stand together, but an obligation to work tirelessly to unite our country and raise the awareness that democracy is sacred. It requires constant care, respect, careful listening, integrity, and honor, and holds the promise for better days ahead. But no individual or political party can do that alone. We must do that together.

All the more so, we cannot ignore the abhorrent symbols that were displayed by yesterday's protestors. Some were prominently displayed on the grounds of the Capitol and some even breached its rotunda, chambers, and offices. They included nooses and swastikas. Some were carrying Confederate flags. Some wore clothing that were labeled NSC131, which is a neo-Nazi organization, and posted on social media: "The U.S. Capitol is now a 131 Zone." Protestors wore shirts displaying "6MWE – 6 Million Weren't Enough." Anti-government militias were there who openly preach the desire for another civil war. And while those are only a few of the repugnant organizations represented by yesterday's violence, there were also men wearing *tzitzit* destroying property and inciting others to do the same.

Tzitzit – A symbol of the 613 mitzvot in the Torah, a reminder of faith, a representation of every Jew's responsibility to take a journey towards holiness, and a commitment that perhaps is best summarized by Rabbi Tarfon's teaching, "We are not required to finish the work, but we must not absolve ourselves from it." That means above anything else, our examples pave the way for the future.

This is not a time in our history to say, "this is not my problem" or "someone else will do the needed work." This is not a time to blame political parties of opposing views. This is the time that we lead by example and model for the generations still to come that each of us holds the ability and promise to make an incredible positive difference for our country and the world. Each of us can do that.

We can inspire, lead, help, grow, learn, change, and improve. "*Im lo achshav, amatai – If not now, when?*"

Our country needs us.

Our future needs us.

And we need each other.

Untold Stories
Rabbi Jeremy Winaker

January 6 7:14pm

I am shocked. I am pained...by so much, including the role of racism. Of course, I am.

I am also keenly aware that I am overwhelmed and need time to process, to sit with my shock and awe.

As an ambivert (both introvert and extrovert), I can come out now and say, it is okay not to have words yet. It is okay to have feelings and to need to sit with them. If you are like me or if you are all introvert, I will be here tomorrow and the next day and the day after to read your words and to listen to you, too.

January 7 10:16am

The stories we tell matter. Stories tell us where we fit in, what we stand for, and by extension who is in and who is out.

For too long, some stories in our society have gone untold or ignored and, more recently, other very dangerous ones have been abetted and amplified.

There are a number of stories to tell about yesterday's insurrection during the certification of the electoral college votes. One more framing comment: Sen. Mitt Romney said the following last night, "No Congressional-led audit will ever convince those voters, particularly when the President will continue to claim that the election was stolen. The best way we can show respect for the voters who are upset is by telling them the truth. That is the burden, and the duty, of leadership." I think it is crucial to name one aspect of the truth he mentioned: it is far less about "Truth" than about SAYING WHAT SOMEONE DOES NOT WANT TO HEAR IN A WAY THAT THEY WILL. That is when a new truth emerges. Here are some things that some of us have not wanted to hear:

1) This President and/or his enablers expressed white supremacy by over-protecting federal buildings during the BLM protests this summer and failing to protect the Capitol during yesterday's protest.

2) Many of Trump's most ardent supporters and many more of those who voted for him were left behind by globalization's economic effects and a concurrent lack of a national story within it.

3) Trump's supporters include many "elites," namely Senators Cruz and Hawley. Everyone should wonder what their goals are given that they know fact from fiction and actively manipulate both.

4) Our children have drilled sheltering in place because of "active shooters." Congress now knows exactly what that is about. Congress can pass laws to make it harder for TERRORISTS to get guns or to bring them into schools or other buildings.

5) White men (and women) rioting with firearms and invading the Capitol are not protesters. They are terrorists. To say otherwise is to perpetuate racism.

6) Yes, thugs can also refer to white people. Finally, the word applied to people who are not black men.

7) In the face of terror, it is important to make the point that society/business/government will go on doing its work; Israel has long exemplified this response.

8) Terror also needs to be addressed by more than moving on. Yes, some senators removed their objections to electoral college votes in light of the day's events. Not enough was said or done yet to demonstrate that the terrorist insurrection was not okay.

9) American history is littered with cases of white supremacist lawlessness and/or acting "above the law" that not only went unpunished, but was tolerated (for example, Wilmington, North Carolina in 1898).

10) A number of "unity services" and "faith calls" took place last night. The events of yesterday beg for the kind of wider perspective religion often provides (yes, religion can also be too narrow). We will need visible leaders coming across apparent divides to help us see what binds us together. Those stories will need to become dominant to change the direction of our societal tribalism (that predates 2016).

Think about the stories you do not like to hear or to listen to. Who or what do you shut out? To tell others what they may not want to hear, we have to practice listening to stories we have ignored/downplayed/brushed off.

I have often been confronted by someone who is not going to change their mind by any fact I might present.

Nevertheless, I have succeeded in changing their attitude by being curious, asking them to tell me more, and stating clearly that I want things to be better (setting aside my own ideas for how to improve them until after I hear the other). It is HARD work.

The rabbis tell us that God listened to the Israelites' cries of suffering in their slavery to Pharaoh and did nothing. Only when Moses turned aside from his royal retinue and took note of the Israelites did God decide to leave God's court to talk with Moses, beginning the Exodus story.

We cannot wait to start listening, to start saying what needs to be said, and to act upon it.

After Georgia,
After Insurrection
Rabbi Rachel Timoner

I felt the need to speak to you this morning, though it was not part of our original plan. I felt the need to speak to you in the week that the Reverend Doctor Raphael Warnock, John Lewis's pastor, the pastor of Ebenezer Baptist Church, (where Martin Luther King Jr was baptized, gave his first sermon at age 19, and served as pastor for the rest of his life) became the first Black senator from the state of Georgia. I felt the need to speak to you in the week that Jon Ossoff, John Lewis's intern, became the first Jewish senator from the State of Georgia. In the week when a Black-Jewish alliance in the South won the Senate for the Democrats, making our synagogue member, Chuck Schumer, the first Jewish Senate Majority Leader, making the first Black-Indian Woman Vice President, Kamala Harris, the tie-breaker in the Senate, and saving America from the depraved current leadership of the Republican party. I need to make sure we all know and saw that Ossoff and Warnock campaigned together, backed each other up and defended each other against racist and antisemitic attacks, and they won together, in the state where Stacey Abrams showed us the future of democracy.

I felt the need to speak to you in the week when White Supremacy threw a temper tantrum, in which White Supremacy, as it faces existential threat, tried to prevent the peaceful transfer of power in the United States. It tried to block democracy, as it's been doing effectively for most of our history. Because democracy will be the demise of White Supremacy, and Georgia is the harbinger of that demise.

We're going to remember this week for the rest of our lives.

Now, while we are shaken by the very real dangers unleashed and on display this week, the 6MWE t-shirts, which stand for 6 Million Were Not Enough, the Camp Auschwitz t-shirts, which need no explanation, the gallows with the noose erected near the Capitol, the Confederate Flags waved inside the Capitol and hung yesterday on the Museum of Jewish Heritage here in New York, the fact that 45 percent of Republicans polled said they think the siege on the Capitol building was justified, the fact that the insurrectionists and all of the white nationalists and many of that 45% are armed to the teeth, the facts that are coming out now that there were many off duty police officers in that crowd and that it seems they had help from inside, the fact that this has now been done and we have all seen it, making a coup and violent insurrection something imaginable in this country, the fact that four years of the steady dismantling of democracy has taken an immeasurable toll, a toll that we can't even fully perceive, all of this is actually dangerous.

But I want to remind us that all of this is happening, the entire last four years, because we are winning. Because the movements for justice, dignity, and equality are winning. And despite the Trump presidency, we're still winning. The Biden-Harris administration will be the most diverse administration in American history. And they cannot stop this forward movement. No one can stop this forward movement.

I want to remind us of how well our democracy is holding up against relentless assault. And that is because of grassroots organizers like the Stacey Abrams's of the world, the everyday activists like the 10,000 people who participated in Get Organized Brooklyn with us here at CBE, and the hundreds of thousands of people who got out the vote, and the movement builders and the guardians of civil society, and because of journalists, and fearless truth-tellers. In 2016 we knew that this man was a fascist, though we were afraid to use the word and said more polite things like autocrat or authoritarian. We knew. We were warned by the Masha Gessens and the Timothy Snyders that our democracy was in danger and it could die on his watch. We knew that he would never voluntarily relinquish power. This could have been so much worse. We could have not had an election at all this year. It could have not been fair. He could have won. We could have had an actual coup, or an actual civil war. Those things are still, of course, possible, but here we are, 11 days before the inauguration, and this was the coup? It was pretty feeble. It was a desecration of our Capitol building and our government and our values, but no one was actually afraid that the insurrectionists would succeed.

Rabbi Yitz Greenberg teaches that the Jewish people live in a dialectic between the reality and the dream. The dream is the messianic vision, a world of justice, dignity, equality and harmony for all life. We are to commit ourselves to the dream, and to see ourselves as responsible for it, never giving up. But we're also never to look away from the reality, even when it is very ugly.

In the parasha this week, Moses sees a bush on fire but not consumed. He stops and turns aside to look. In Shemot Rabba (1:27), the rabbis suggest that the reason God chose Moses to call at the burning bush was because this was not the first time that Moses turned aside to look. "*The Holy Blessed One said: 'You left aside your business and went to see the sorrow of Israel, and acted toward them as brothers act.'*" When, at the bush, Moses turned aside to see, "*The Holy Blessed One saw Moses, who turned aside to see the burdens of his brothers.*"

It was Moses's willingness to turn aside to see the suffering and oppression around him in Egypt-- the injustice, the hate -- that merited him being chosen to lead the people out of Egypt.

This week we saw the reality of white supremacy, we saw the extreme edge of the 74 million Americans who voted for Donald Trump. We saw where we are as a nation. We saw that the palace is on fire, our society, our world is ablaze with white supremacy, and there is no way to make our democracy whole without looking squarely at it, as Rabbi Sharon Brous taught us, to either remove or pay for the stolen beam at the foundation of our house, meaning that the edifice of our society was built on the theft of human lives and freedom. And in the Talmud, the Rabbis consider, when you find that your house was built on a stolen beam, whether you must take the house apart and remove the beam or whether you can simply pay restitution for the theft.

The white supremacy on display this week was another reminder that there is no way to avoid taking account of all of the theft that undergirds our society, and the ideology and systems that have been maintained ever since, from slavery until now. We can look away and pretend it isn't real, but if we ever want to heal, if we ever want a whole democracy, we must turn aside from our business and see.

This is what it is to be a Jew, to live right inside of all of the ugliness of reality, to see it squarely, and also to hold on to the dream. Civil rights elder Vincent Harding described a river that is always flowing from the reality to the dream. The river is sometimes frozen, he said, and the flow is hidden under the surface. Other times the river is turbulent and rapid. But it is always flowing. The river is inevitable. The river cannot be stopped. We are not the resistance, Michelle Alexander taught us, we are the river. A mixed multitude who, in a few weeks of Torah will make our way to freedom, linking arms together, across all of our differences, moving always toward justice, equality, dignity, harmony for all life, toward freedom.

Let us turn aside to see the reality. Let us not be afraid. Let us hold on to the dream and have trust and faith that it is coming. Let us remember that we are the river, and together, we're flowing, we're on our way there.

How can we heal America? Look to the Egyptians who aided Moses.

Rabbi Elliot Cosgrove

Shocking as this past week's storming of the Capitol by domestic terrorists may have been, it was not a surprise. There is a direct line between the actions and personalities of last Wednesday and those of Charlottesville in August of 2017.

Trump's video, issued while rioters were in the Capitol, telling them "We love you. You're very special" was just a new "Some very fine people on both sides."

The Nazi slogans brandished last week in D.C. were a natural evolution on the Charlottesville chants of "Jews will not replace us."

We have seen this coming for years. I am reminded of the Hemingway line in reply to the question "How did you go bankrupt?"

His answer: "Two ways. Gradually, and then suddenly."

Civil society does not unravel all at once. There is no one moment when conscience crumbles and dissent dies.

According to the Torah, when the Children of Israel first followed Joseph into Egypt, they held an important place in Egyptian society and in the Egyptian imagination. But then "A new king arose over Egypt who did not know Joseph." For whatever reason — likely because he was threatened — this new Pharaoh systematically "othered" the Israelites, played on Egyptians' fears to transform a country once defined by "us," into an "us" and "them."

According to the rabbis, Pharaoh's shrewd strategy had a clear method. First he worked to change the cultural climate; then the laws; then the very definition of truth. He was subtle, moving so gradually that when he issued the decree to enslave the Israelites and kill their male children, it was met with little — if any — objection. Each stage of his plan normalized what would have otherwise been unconscionable.

But social norms do not come undone exclusively because of the designs of one man. It took the complicity of many others for Pharaoh's strategy to be realized. Maybe "Joe Egyptian" thought the bile Pharaoh was spewing could be shrugged off as the indulgent excesses of a charismatic leader: "That's just Pharaoh being Pharaoh."

"All right, I don't like the guy, but he is good for Egypt," he might have thought. "He projects strength, and just look at all the construction: These pyramids not only boost the economy but give us a point of shared pride." At a certain point, it gets uncomfortable to take a stand, and be the odd one out. The line between self-interest and self-preservation is not a clear one.

We must learn from the Torah's account of what happened in Egypt. Pharaoh undoubtedly had his own cohort of true believers. But more consequential were those who facilitated his worst policies, those who were indifferent, complicit or concerned only with their own well-being.

Just as we must learn from those who enabled Pharaoh, so too we can learn from those actions that led to the Israelites' liberation. That process began with the decision of midwives to disobey Pharaoh's decree: it teaches that moral courage is within everyone's reach. So, too, it should not be missed that Pharaoh's daughter saved Moses, teaching that no matter how close one is to the throne — even as close as Pharaoh's daughter — it is still possible to act with empathy and conscience. The fact that Moses risked and lost everything by striking down an Egyptian in the process of assaulting an Israelite slave affirms that moral leadership comes not by protecting self-interest, but by protecting the interest of the person who has no one else to protect them.

What is the lesson for an America in pain? Redemption happens step-by-step, one upstanding citizen at a time, making decisions small and large to push back. It is really not more complicated than that. May we all learn from the events of the past week gone by and strive to step up to the calling of the hour.

The Heart Breaks Open
Rabbi Lisa Gelber

So many questions in the midst of the Capitol Riots, insurrection, attempt to obliterate democracy. Spelling words piled like bricks to create store cities of constriction and enslavement to hatred and bile. The pain of young ears and eyes and heart spilled like dressing onto the dinner plate.

Mommy, I am so nice, but I can be cold.
Cold, my empathetic child? I see your broken heart.

Trump is ruthless. Are the senators afraid of him? Are his children embarrassed? Was anyone hurt today? The questions spill over like a bubbling fountain or running faucet. And then. It's their funeral you know. The heart closes just a bit, hardening like Pharaoh's. Let's see who gets COVID19. You know, someone will have to tend to the injured and dead. That's true.

The heart breaks open and pumps pain like oxygenated blood cells running through the body. We breathe in love and beans and rice and cheese. We turn to the television, a running stream of new words and numbers like impeachment and 25. Climbing into bed, we call the angels forth to stand for what is holy, strengthen our resolve for change, envision the future and pray for healing of hearts and minds and souls and animals. The sun will rise tomorrow.

May the questions cut through the bonds of slavery and lead us to a promised land.

Curses, Foiled Again
Rabbi Jack Moline

"Cursed be the one who will not uphold the terms of this teaching and observe them – and all the people shall say, "amen.'" - Deuteronomy 27:26

Ah, the power of the crowd. If you have ever been a part of one, you know what I mean. You go to a home-town game of your favorite sports team and the energy of thousands of fans, cheering and booing, adds to the experience. Seeing a comedy in a crowded theater (remember that?) makes the laughter more contagious (and the ill-timed silences more profound). And when the familiar opening riff of a rock-and-roll classic blasts from the stage, you, along with everyone around you, are born to run.

I leave it to scientists to explain the physical reactions that are generated by being a part of such a collective experience. I myself can report both as participant and as observer that there is an undeniable energy that emanates from an inspired crowd. The question is, what inspires them?

Back when I was a congregational rabbi, I was glad to exploit this group mentality. When I was skilled and fortunate enough to compose a lesson that engaged people, I could feel the intensity and perceive, when I brought a teaching or a sermon to conclusion, what my wife called a "quality of silence" that vibrated through the sanctuary. I had the privilege to work with a cantor whose voice had the same effect on worshipers. And on those occasions when we integrated our presentations – for example, one memorable time that I discussed, and she sang Leonard Cohen's "Hallelujah" – the effect was so electric it likely violated the prohibitions of labor on sacred Jewish holidays.

But I have seen that collective energy used for less holy purposes. A couple of summers back, when we were not prisoners of a virus, I stood on the desolate parade ground on the outskirts of Nuremberg looking up at the concrete platform that hosted evil incarnate before I was born. The quality of silence in that place was of a distinctly different nature, still whispering the deafening shouts of (mostly) young (mostly) men in adulation of someone asking them to do what, in private reflection, they would most certainly know was wrong.

Somewhere between these two extremes are political rallies in this our democracy.

My college roommate, still my best friend, refuses to participate in the chanting that is so often a part of rallies. He can't stand the exercise. While people around us were being led in "Hey hey, ho ho, [political figure] has got to go" he would just be shaking his head. I think of him whenever, in my capacity as the leader of an advocacy group, I attend a demonstration and get handed a printed list of chants to lead when I conclude whatever brief remarks I am asked to give. Rather than choosing to channel Country Joe McDonald ("gimme an F…"), I mostly decline, using my age as an excuse.

Plus, I have begun to see how dangerous this chanting business can be when the crowd is encouraged by a manipulative speaker. I guess "four more years" is innocuous enough, but "lock her up" or "stop the steal" encourages and justifies the diminishment of the social order and the humanity of those who disagree.

Reading a bill of particulars and asking people to shout a verdict is mob rule. It may be as old as the Bible, but it has a decidedly unholy purpose. It is one step away from the townspeople grabbing torches and marching on Baron von Frankenstein's mansion, which makes for great entertainment but very bad – and very illegal – public behavior.

There is one thing that commends riling up a crowd and it is this: the Riler-in-Chief of the moment is face to face with the Rilees. The speaker must take responsibility for what comes out of their mouth, and there is collective witness (and most often a record) of what they said. Those who succumb to herd impunity cannot deny its origins. The amen-activity is attached by a string that is fixed at one end to the speaker and the other end to the actor.

It is different than the anonymous (or, at least, mitigated) rabble rousing of social media, where Q can dodge the onus by remaining Anon.

And it is because of this last technological innovation that I understand Moses reciting the imprecations and demanding the affirming chant at the end. The feedback is immediate, the effect is electrifying and the message – in this case – is essentially moral. Yet I cannot help but think that if Moses had thought it through, he would have rallied the crowd around blessings.

Reminders
Rabbi Avram Mlotek

It unfolded like a movie except it wasn't fictional and none of us knew how the story would end. A mob of people descending on our nation's capital. Tweets and pictures painting a scene: the Senate floor in session only to be interrupted in a most vicious way.

Watching the damage unfold, I thought: this is what happens after four years of a president who instigates, who stokes mistrust in democratic institutions, who maniacally lies, and does whatever is in his best interest. It was a *busha*, a shameful embarrassment, that an Onion headline saying "Serbia Deploys Peacekeeping Forces to U.S." felt so *shayakh*, appropriate that day.

For a president who revels in his supposed credence to "law and order," I couldn't help but wonder what happened that day? How is it that riot police were armed and ready when a Black Lives Matter protest took the streets but when White men and women stormed our nation's capital, they managed to enter into the most sacred chambers of American democracy? The rioters that day did not need protection: their White skin was enough of a shield that allowed them to put up their feet on a congresswoman's desk, to stand where presidents stand during the State of the Union. What do we spend trillions of dollars on our defense for if not for riotous, coup-like behavior?

And to my fellow Jews, I felt compelled to cry: *Yidn - a vort*, a word! Remember this man who wore a Camp Auschwitz T-Shirt. Remember the assault on an Israeli reporter that happened today too. Remember the shirts which stated 6MWE standing for "6 million wasn't enough." These are the people the president said "we love you" to when he instructed them to go home (after telling them to show up hours before). These are the decent people on the other side the president reminded us about in Charlottesville.

Speaking with my grandmother that day, a Holocaust refugee from Berlin, she said to me, "I don't recognize the America I came to as a little girl." It was a painful and tragic day for these reasons and more. And still, I remain hopeful. Because a state that once lynched Black men that day also elected their first Black senator along with their first Jewish senator. Because Congress continued ratifying election results only hours after the debacle took place. But it was a reminder too - if ever we needed one - that our Democracy is precious and fragile.

Confederate Flags

Rabbi Rachel Kobrin

There are a lot of photos that have gone viral from Wednesday — mostly horrible and frightening photos of men carrying confederate flags and wearing terrifying antisemitic clothing.

I'm mentioning them, because I am imagining most of us have seen them and were horrified by them, but I actually don't want to focus on these images.

I want to talk about another photo that also went viral — a picture of the senate aids, young women, carrying the ballots to the house chamber to be counted. When the picture was first seen, people thought these women were carrying the ballots out — saving the ballots from the terrorists who had infiltrated the Capitol building. But it actually doesn't matter whether it was before our after the attack — what is compelling is the image itself — brave, strong young women holding in their hands the future of our democracy.

One of these women is Brennon Leach. I happen to know that because I know her dad - he served for years in the Pennsylvania legislature — and he generously invited my friend Rabbi Andi Merow and me to join his family in the select seating area when Hilary Clinton spoke in Philly four years ago on the evening before the election. I haven't seen Brennon since that evening, but I was thrilled to see that viral photo of her carrying those ballots, cementing her role as a vital participant in saving our democracy.

Our parashah tells the story of the midwives — women who are told by Pharoah, their wicked ruler, to throw the Jewish babies into the water. But these midwives do not listen. They don't listen to the ignorant and racist voice of their political leader. Instead they lead a movement of civil disobedience — listening to the cries of the babies on the birth stool, as those newborns take in their first breath of life. These are the cries that inspire the midwives to be leaders--to stand up against tyranny and hate responding with bravery and love.

And then we meet Bat Paroh — Pharaoh's daughter. She knows to turn away from the evil ways of her father the minute she "sees the cries" of Moshe in the water. The text says that she *sees* the cries — an interesting word choice, as opposed to hearing. We know that when our Torah switches the senses — using "see" when "hear" is what we might have expected — that the Torah is trying to emphasize a point. When Bat Paroh sees these cries, she is jolted from her comfortable reality, she sees the pain, and she knows she must respond. She cannot remain silent. And so she reaches into the water and saves Moses — doing what she can to create shelter and share love.

Together, these biblical women model what it means to walk in this world with bravery and purpose and to truly hear, see, and act.

Really hearing and seeing right now is painful. Being present means being courageous enough to recognize the realities of the white supremacy on which this nation was built and which has invaded the hearts and minds of people in this nation in very concrete ways. It means seeing the reality that we have been living with a president who has fueled this hatred for four long years, stirring the pot and leading people to the terrifying acts we saw on Wednesday. In two weeks' time, or possibly sooner, Donald Trump will no longer hold the office of president. But his followers — the ones who appeared in those terrifying photos, as well as those who have bought into his rhetoric or hid behind excuses for refusing to call him out — they will still exist. We cannot ignore this reality. For too long, too many people have shamefully looked the other way as hatred was provoked in this country, fearful of speaking truth to power. Silence should never have been an option.

The midwives and Bat Paroh model a certain kind of holy action that is vital in this hour — hearing and seeing the results of four years of Trump's destructive statements and policies; hearing and seeing the white supremacy and antisemitism within our country; and hearing and seeing the cries of those oppressed by these institutions and reaching out our hands and responding. Listening for these cries will challenge us to partner with one another. To build coalitions. To work for change. Thankfully, there are millions of people who want to be doing this work with us. Look at Georgia — a state that carries the insidious scar of being the place where a Jewish man and many black people were lynched — and in Georgia, this past week, the first black man and the first Jew were elected to the senate. They partnered and supported one another to make this possible. And through the leadership of the righteous Stacey Abrams, and others who worked tirelessly in Georgia, they partnered to fulfill a dream of what America can be. As Reverend Warnock said — "The other day, because this is America, the 82-year-old hands that used to pick somebody else's cotton went to the polls and picked her youngest son to be a United States senator." THAT is the America we believe in — and that is the America we will continue to birth.

And I think THAT is a reason that the image of Bennan and her fellow interns carrying those ballots went viral. Young women carrying the democratic process in their hands — Shifra and Puah, helping to birth a new era for our nation, shepherding the ballots and declaring "evil will not win. Lies will not stand. We will renew our commitment to being a nation built on the values of truth and justice." That is an image that represents what we dream of — an image that our hearts need so desperately right now.

A little later in our parshah, Moses stands by the burning bush and God cries to him — "Moshe! Moshe!" And our rabbis teach — this really is a substantial cry from God. Different from "Avraham, Avraham" in the story of the Akeda, where the angel pauses between the 2 pronouncements of Abraham's name. "Moshe Moshe" is said in a rushed fashion — God is truly crying to Moshe.

And likewise, I dare say. God is now crying to us. And God is begging us to listen, to see, and to respond — just like the midwives and Bat Paroh did. Using our compassion and wisdom to pull our nation out of the water and save it.

When Rev Warnock won his election, he quoted psalm 30: "We may lie down weeping in the night, but joy comes in the morning."

That psalm ends with the words that we sang at the start of our service — *You turn my mourning into dancing — my sackcloth into robes of joy.*

As we end this week and begin then next, I am betting many of us are mixed with emotions of grief and hope, of anger and faith. Judaism demands that in moments like this we remember those midwives and the daughter of Pharaoh — and that we gain inspiration from those senate interns — and that we refuse to despair.

Yesterday Brennan shared with me "The chaos on Wednesday was something I will never forget, but I'm very grateful to be safe now and to have a new administration on its way... perhaps there is light at the end of the tunnel."

In my heart, I hear God crying with us for the calamity of this past week and reminding us not to despair. A new day is dawning. And through listening, seeing, and sacred political action, we can release the darkness, and welcome the sunrise.

The Power of Words
Rabbi Lisa Gelber

I'm back by my window, sitting in the sun of a new day. What a relief the sun rose this morning and that each day God creates the world anew, as our daily liturgy reminds us. The sun and cloudless sky as I write on Thursday morning seems hopeful, but it cannot erase the images from Wednesday which feel seared into my brain and being. I fear the photo of domestic terrorists scaling the wall around the Capitol will be used in a movie and take me right back to the day on which reprehensible action aimed to disrupt our democracy and resulted in the death of 5 souls.

Years ago, when studying *Schenk vs. US* in my High School Constitutional Law Class with Werner Feig (whose archetype and name found its way into the television series *The West Wing*), I was introduced to the notion of "clear and present danger" in relation to speech. The power of *not crying fire in a crowded theater* cannot be underestimated. Words have power. The storming of our nation's capital demonstrated the way in which *language designed to promote disinformation and incite violence*[2] can upend lawful expression of democracy.

From the very beginning of our Torah, we learn the power of the word. Only 3 verses into the Torah, we read, "*Vayomer Elohim y'hi or, vay'hi or / God said, 'Let there be light,' and there was light.*"[3] According to our formational narrative, the speech of the holy one creates light, pulling order out of chaos, enabling us to see, distinguish and discern. These abilities are listed among our morning blessings and help set the intention of how we live our lives every single day. In this week's *parasha*, as we begin the story of our experience as slaves in the book of Exodus, we are again reminded of

---

[2] A comment by Jonathan Greenblatt, CEO, Anti-Defamation League.
[3] Genesis 1:3

the potency of words as Moses names his son Gershom - גר שם/*ger sham, for he said, I have been a stranger in a foreign land* (Exodus 2:22). Moses invests his child with the experience of his father. We can imagine them speaking over dinner about how and why they received their names[4] and what it means to carry that legacy in the way in which one introduces oneself and one's story.

In September, I framed our new Jewish year as invitation to chapters of love, writing, 5781 is תש"פא – an acronym for תתחדש שנת פרקי אהבה - *may this be a year of loving chapters*. Not long after that, the Capitol welcomed Supreme Court Justice Ruth Bader Ginsburg z'l as the first woman and first Jewish person honored to lay in state at the U.S. Capitol. Statuary Hall was a space for sacred words of holy remembrance. They reminded us of the power of words that loved law and democracy, justice and the American people.

In this new year 2021, I did not imagine myself feeling like a stranger in a strange land, watching the Capitol building transformed into a place of unrest, unmasked bullies taking selfies in the hall, our nation's elected representatives barricaded behind doors, under tables and desks with gas-masks. The House Chaplain offered words of prayer before they were whisked away, bringing comfort in time of distress and also raising up the serious nature of what was unfolding in the sacred house of democracy.

Like Moses, we too are on a journey from slavery to freedom. It is on all of us to take these steps into the new year seriously. The Talmud reminds us *kol arevim zeh bazeh/each one of us is responsible for the other*.[5] We don't have to agree. We must see ourselves as responsible for one another. The book of Proverbs is wise and clear, *Death and life are in the power of the tongue*.[6] As we take hold of this new

---

[4] Also see Ex. 2:10
[5] Shavuot 39a
[6] Proverbs 18:21

secular year, let us use our words to build up brick by brick, bring justice, embrace democracy and tell the next chapters of the story of our country as ones of generosity, responsibility, commitment and compassion.

May each day this year be better than the one that came before.

May God and we bless America.

It is crucial that we allow our speech to be restorative

Rabbi Marc Labowitz

To those of us, who, like me, have watched aghast and appalled as rights have been turned into wrongs and wrongs into rights, who have wondered out loud, 'What is happening to our beloved country, and why?'

As though we were living in an era of individual isolation punctuated by moments bursting with violence, it seems the only times we connected was to shout at one another. And I'm not sure if our isolation is helping pacify what could've been worse or hurting what might've been more productive exchanges on the streets of America.

And so, when dumb-founded - as we have been during many shared moments throughout this year - we turn to the writings of our people:

> To everything there is a season,
>> and a time to every purpose under the heaven;
> A time to break down,
>> and a time to build up;
> A time to weep, and a time to laugh;
>> a time to mourn, and a time to dance;
> A time to cast away stones,
>> and a time to gather stones together; a time to embrace,
>> and a time to refrain from embracing;
> A time to seek, and a time to lose;
>> a time to keep, and a time to cast away;
> A time to tear, and a time to mend;
>> a time to be silent, and a time to speak;
> A time to love, and a time to hate;
>> a time of war, and a time of peace. (Ecclesiastes 3)

One could argue that this Holy Scripture simultaneously inspires violence, chaos and hatred as well as order, peace and love. Some will read it as an invitation to pick up stones and throw them, while others will gather stones and build a house or clear a field. And that's what King Solomon is expressing: Everyone's interpretation of the purpose in the moment is different, because everyone's interpretation of the truth is different.

King David espoused that there are as many truths as there are blades of grass when he wrote : 'And the truth will grow from the earth.' (Ps. 85:12) Because, although there may appear to be only be one Divine truth, there are as many interpretations of it as there are people expressing it. So, it will have to grow out of the earth, a blade of grass at a time, if need be, until we reach consensus.

As a rabbi, I'm finding it ever more challenging to find remedial words; to express what will heal and uplift the mood of the country whose political climate is at a boiling point.

Now, more than ever, it is crucial that we allow our speech to be restorative.

The Prophet Isaiah writes:

> 'Comfort ye, comfort ye, my people' says your God. 'Speak to the heart of Jerusalem ...' (Isa. 40:1-2)

It was God telling the prophet, 'If you have a message for people, even a message of hope and comfort, you will have to speak to their hearts. When people are wounded enough, plain talk won't cut through their pain and isolation. It must be restorative speech.'

When Ecclesiastes says there is a time to speak, he did not mean a time for speeches. He meant there will be a time for us to speak to the heart of our fellow Americans. I know that the moment for us to begin speaking to one another once again is coming, because things will eventually calm down.

I believe in our democratic republic and I believe in the power of dialogue. For it is dialogue which ensures that the ties binding us together are stronger than those that would tear us apart.

But we must choose the moment for dialogue carefully, for there is a 'time to speak.'

The Talmud teaches that one does not try to appease someone while they are still enraged.[7]

And when someone allows you to appease them, it proves not only that you want a relationship with them, but that they want the same. I believe it is the desire of the soul of this country that we restore our civil unity, that we speak to the heart of our neighbor, 'You've been in my life and I want you to be in my life in the future.'

We don't have a choice. We don't have another option. We live in the same country.

Ecclesiastes also asserts there is 'a time to be silent.' לחשות is the word used instead of לשתוק, indicating that sometimes our silence says more than words can. In dialogue it's important to listen and allow people to express themselves for that is also way to communicate to the heart. By listening to someone else's heart being expressed. This requires great patience and fortitude especially if the ideologies expressed oppose your own.

Strangely, Ecclesiastes has a time for everything under the

---

[7] Berachot 7a

sun, but he does not mention a time for prayer. Possibly, because there's no time which does not call for prayer. Whether a prayer is spoken out loud or reflected upon quietly, if we're looking for common ground, then prayer is that shared space. In prayer, we are still united.

The definition of a civilized country is one in which there is a peaceful transfer of power. It is literally the definition of a democracy. But if we are no longer able, as Democrats, Republicans and independent Americans, to manage such a thing, then this is certainly a time for prayer.

Let us pray for great leadership and encourage its influence on our body-politic. Let us hope that we learn the lessons of this period. And let us pray for the strength to hold fast, to stand by our ideals, and remain as a beacon of resolution and faith in the future of our common well-being and happiness. Let us pray for the patience to do the right thing while we wait for better days.

We have weathered worse, and are the better for it, for we are the solid, dependable fiber from which the fabric of this country has been woven over the centuries.

Winners and Losers
Rabbi Annie Tucker

There are some stories so bizarre that you just can't make them up, and the following one is told by authors Steven Levitt and Stephen Dubner in their bestselling book, <u>Freakonomics</u>. In 1958, a young couple named the Lanes, living in a Harlem housing project, gave birth to a baby boy. The Lanes had several children already but felt particularly optimistic about the new arrival. To convey their high hopes for their son, they chose a name befitting of the success they felt sure he was to achieve. They named their infant Winner. Three years later, the Lanes gave birth to another child and again went through the important process of selecting a name. For reasons that are not entirely clear, inspiration struck the Lanes differently this time or perhaps they simply had an odd sense of humor. Whatever the explanation, the little boy's name was chosen. He was called Loser.

As it turns out, Loser Lane was able to rise above his difficult beginnings and beat the odds with much success. He received a scholarship to prep school, graduated from college, and went on to join the NYPD where he eventually became a detective and then a sergeant. As for his brother? By the time he was in his mid-forties, Winner Lane had been arrested nearly three dozen times for crimes ranging from burglary to domestic violence, trespassing to resisting arrest. As Levitt and Dubner write,

> "These days, Loser and Winner barely speak. The father who named them is no longer alive. Clearly, he had the right idea – that naming is destiny ... He [just] must have gotten the boys mixed up" (Freakonomics, p. 180).

While many of us will giggle to hear the peculiar story of the Lane children, perhaps we should not be so quick to dismiss the questions raised by this strange tale. How much *do* our names control our destiny? What *is* the relationship between what we are called and who we are called to be in this world? What, ultimately, makes someone a Winner in the grand scheme of life and what renders someone instead a Loser?

In many ways, the early narratives of our Torah read a bit like the Lane family saga where children are constantly being given names that reflect their circumstances – either real or aspirational. Yitzhak is named for his mother's laughter and Moshe for being drawn from the water. The names of Leah's first three children reflect her hopes that she will regain her husband's affection, and the names of Joseph's two boys reflect the healing that has finally come after the painful difficulties of childhood. Avram and Sarai's names are changed to Abraham and Sarah in recognition of their new covenant with the Divine, and Jacob's name moves from Ya'akov – reflective of his painful relationship with brother, Esau – to Yisrael – reflective of his ability to both struggle and prevail with God and man. The Bible teaches us that names have meaning. While they may not always foretell one's destiny, they convey a great deal about from where one has come.

Looked at in this way, it is not surprising that the second book of the Torah, the beginning of our journey as a people which we start today, is called *Shemot* – Names. If what we are called conveys our roots – our origins and beginnings – then there is no better place to launch our epic tale of slavery and deliverance than with a reminder that the Jewish nation about to be born is the legacy of a Jewish family, the 12 sons of Jacob, whose unique experiences encountering God and one another have prepared them well for the adventure that they're about to undertake. By beginning with names we are reminded that a community is ultimately made up of individuals, each of us important in our own right and not merely a measure of population growth. Names remind us that this national journey is deeply personal, that each of us should read ourselves into the story of our people rather than simply imagining it in the abstract.

While the parasha named Shemot begins with names, however, it also contains some striking omissions when it comes to the very same. Not one of the pharaohs of Egypt is named in our Torah portion, not even the one ultimately responsible for dooming the Israelites to slavery. Similarly, Bat Pharaoh – the daughter of Pharaoh who saves baby Moses from the banks of the Nile – also remains nameless throughout our narrative, described not as a distinct individual but rather as her father's child. Even Moses' own parents and sister – individuals whose well-known names are later revealed – remain anonymous in this parasha which simply reads: "*Vayelech ish mibeit Levi vayikach et bat Levi* –A certain man of the house of Levi went and married a Levite woman" (Exodus 2:1). For a Torah portion named for naming, Parashat Shemot seems curiously lacking in this regard.

The editors of the *Etz Hayim Humash* offer an explanation for this strange omission, suggesting that the reason that Moses' parents' names are not revealed to us until next week is to teach us that the particulars of this individual family are irrelevant but rather that *any* parent can give rise to a great leader. They emphasize that what makes Moses exceptional is not pre-destination or circumstances of birth but rather an accumulation of human choices made by the man himself and by those closest to him. Baby Moses does not become "Moshe Rabbenu" – our great teacher and prophet – simply by dint of conception. He becomes Moshe Rabbenu through a mother and sister willing to risk their lives to ensure his safety. He becomes Moshe Rabbenu through a Pharaoh's daughter with super-human powers of compassion and two Hebrew midwives brave enough to defy royal orders. And he becomes Moshe Rabbenu by displaying moral courage in a place sorely lacking it – standing up for the rights of the oppressed and stepping into the uncomfortable role of leader in order to deliver his people to freedom. Much like the story of Winner and Loser Lane, the Torah is reminding us that our names and our backgrounds are *not* necessarily our destiny; each of us has the ability to chart our own path no matter it is from where we have come. "A certain man of the house of Levi went and married a Levite woman." Any person brave enough to make good choices can similarly be the forebear of redemption.

Rabbi Nahum Sarna, author of the JPS Torah Commentary on Exodus, takes the chumash's idea one step further when he explains that the presence and absence of certain names within our parasha is absolutely deliberate and designed to call attention to those who are significant in the eyes of Tradition and, equally important, those who are not. Perhaps the greatest example of this is the striking juxtaposition between the description of Pharaoh, the most powerful man in all of Egypt, and the description of the Hebrew midwives, women of lowly status who spend their lives ministering to others. While Pharaoh is referred to simply as "a new king who knew not Joseph" – stripped of personal attributes and spoken about only in reference to another, more central figure – the Torah explains that "Pharaoh spoke to the Hebrew midwives, one of whom was named Shifra and the other Puah" (Exodus 1:15). Each of these women is seen as meaningful and distinct, separate from her partner and identified by a proper name. In a story about slavery and redemption, the Bible clearly indicates that what makes a person worthy and powerful is not wealth or military might, the size of one's territory or the fear that one inspires in others. Rather, what makes individuals deserving of a place in history is their morality – their willingness to defy evil and strive for right, their sense of responsibility for the welfare of others, their willingness to sacrifice personal safety and security for the sake of the greater good. How fitting it is that 3300 years after the Exodus we do not mention the name of the tyrant responsible for dooming us to slavery. Yet the names of those who challenged brutality and slaughter will never be forgotten!

Finally, I believe there is one last symbolic element in these names that are named (and unnamed) in Parashat Shemot – a lesson that also serves as a warning about one of our parasha's major themes – human exploitation, tyranny, and genocide. The first step in destroying another people is to dehumanize them – to strip them of their individuality and uniqueness, their identity and their name. It is this kind of de-individuation that led the Nazis to tattoo numbers onto their victims during World War II, robbing them of their distinctiveness. It is also, perhaps, for this reason that Israel's Holocaust Museum is called *Yad va'Shem* – a phrase taken from the verse in Isaiah which indicates that "within my walls a *memorial and a name* shall not be cut off" (Isaiah 56:5). When we allow people to lose their names we risk allowing them to lose their humanity, and the same is also true in reverse – when we stop seeing ourselves as distinct individuals but rather as part of a large, anonymous mass we can come to do terrible things. The absence of a consistent use of names in Shemot is the very first sign that something has begun to go desperately wrong.

Given the horrifying events in our country earlier this week, the lessons of Shemot suddenly feel more relevant than ever. Watching a violent pack of rioters enter the sacred sanctum of the U.S. Capital threatening both our lawmakers and the very notion of democracy itself, we are reminded anew of the dangers that come when people engage in mob mentality – de-individuating both themselves and their victims so as to decrease notions of personal responsibility and numb oneself to any potential harm caused. Incited by a man who bears perhaps the loftiest title in all the world, we are reminded that what ultimately makes persons worthy and significant is not the power they have but how they choose to yield it, not the office they hold but how they use that perch to influence the world either for good or for ill. And seeing the courage of ordinary citizens like the young staffers who had the presence of mind to carry ballot boxes out of the room even as they fled for their life – we are reminded that regular people can easily become heroes, that any brave person willing to make good choices can indeed become the forebear of redemption. As this tragic week comes to an end, we wish comfort and healing to those emotionally and physically wounded by these events and peace and stability upon our country and the proud democracy that it represents. *Ken y'hi ratzon* – May this truly be God's will.

Years ago the Lane children defied expectations by forging life paths opposite from those that had seemingly been cast for them, and the characters of Shemot did much the same. Mighty Pharaoh, with every privilege and luxury at his disposal, showed himself an immoral Loser while a scrappy and courageous band of women won the day through standing up for justice and right. How easy it is to surpass the low opinions of those who underestimate us! May the example of these brave leaders remind us of the possibility for redemption that lies within every family, the qualities that win or lose a person her place in history, and the dangers of ever forgetting a single person's immeasurable humanity – including our own.

A Fragile World
Rabbi Ron Fish

Democracy, like our religious tradition, can embrace many voices and much difference. Its strength is derived from the truth that out of many we become one. The Talmud teaches us that Gods truth has room for divergent, sometimes conflicting voices:

> "Both these and those are the words of the living God." (Eruvin)

Yet democracy and religious faith can be broken.

> "Speech contains within it the power of life and death." (Proverbs)

When leadership misuses that power it recklessly endangers our very civilization. When that speech calls the unhinged to mutiny and violence based upon lies and conspiracy theories, we know the certain outcome.

Today with broken hearts and truly shaken spirits- we are all called upon to be strong and to strengthen one another. The power of the tongue can heal as well. Our leaders must act to heal our country, restore our fractured union and be the source of justice and peace in our world. The gifts we have received from God, and from our ancestors, are surely fragile. They will only endure if we all treasure them. Benjamin Franklin said that our founders bequeathed us a republic, if we can keep it. And the midrash teaches us in that same spirit that our future is in our own hands. We have all been shaken to our core by yesterday's assault upon our shared treasured inheritance. We must all have renewed resolve to do the work of speaking truth, pursing peace and protecting the gifts we dare not take for granted.

"When God created Adam, God took him around the trees of the Garden of Eden, and said to him, 'Look at My works! How beautiful and praiseworthy they are. Everything that I have created I created for you. Take care not to damage and destroy My world, for if you damage it, there is no one to repair it after you."
-Ecclesiastes Rabba

A Shift in the Narrative
Rabbi Aviva Fellman

In Pirkei Avot (3:2), Rabbi Hanina, the vice-high priest, defined what it means to pray for the government when he said: "One should pray for the welfare of the government, as were it not for the fear of the government, every person would swallow their neighbor alive." I surely felt the reality and urgency in needing to pray for our country and our government over the last 36 hours. For some reason, the words that we recite each shabbat in the Prayer For Our Country did not seem sufficient.

And so the day after the attack, I shared the prayerful poem, "Against Domestic Insurrection," written by Alden Solovy, which includes the following:

> Source and Shelter,
> Grant safety and security
> To the people and democracy of the United States of America.
> Protect us from violence, rebellion, intimidation,
> And attempts to seize our government.
> Save us from domestic terror.
> Save us from leaders who cannot say no to attacks
> On our legacy and our future.
> God of nations and history,
> Let truth and justice resound
> To the four corners of the earth.
> Let the light of freedom
> Shine brightly in the halls of power,
> As a beacon of hope
> For every land and every people.

This Shabbat we will begin reading from the book of Shemot (Exodus). There is a shift in the narrative from being about individual families and birthrights to the story of a nation and a people. My hope and prayer is that this moment is similar for our country. I hope and pray that the domestic terrorism that we witnessed yesterday in our nation's capitol and the subsequent responses to it by many elected officials are a sign and start of a more unified future- where concern for the collective is put before the self.

I love the stories of Genesis, but it is time to move forward and step up as a nation.

Lord knows we need to.

We Must Not Take Our Way of Life for Granted

Rabbi Carnie Shalom Rose
Cantor Sharon Nathanson
Rabbi Jeffrey Abraham
Rabbi Neal Rose

Each Shabbat, right before we return our Torah Scrolls to our Holy Ark, we recite a special prayer for our country. In this prayer, we entreat the Almighty to shower blessings upon "those who exercise just and rightful authority" and we fervently pray that the Holy One may continue to "safeguard the ideals and free institutions which are the pride and glory of our country."

Without question, America has been a great source of blessing for the Jewish people. We have enjoyed greater freedoms here in the past century than in almost any other era of Jewish History. We remain confident that the United States of America will weather this current crisis and that the foundations of our democracy remain secure.

However, we must not take our way of life for granted. Each of us, in our own way, must commit to taking responsibility for safeguarding what it is that we love. We must unequivocally condemn the anarchy and mayhem that we witnessed yesterday in our nation's capital and actively promote an immediate resumption of the rule of law.

PHARAOH 2020

Rabbi Dan Ornstein

Raamses picked at his dirty, fraying swag, the result of too many years' anxiety over keeping his power intact. His once bright gold pschent, his double crown, had turned a faded shade of filthy yellow, and the acronym emblazoned on it – four letters, M- E- G- A - was now starting to chip off. M- E- G- A, "Make Egypt Glorious Again," the faltering Pharaoh's once-brash, wildly popular, populist campaign slogan, was quickly being consigned to the garbage heap of the Egyptian public's attention: well…at least half the public. The other half, Raamses' loyal royal base, had long ago been convinced by him that he was their persecuted savior, for whom they should be ready to kill if necessary.

Those same Egyptians, all Egyptians in fact, were rapidly dying from the devastation of successive plagues – pandemics, the boring scientists with their stupid facts called them. But Raamses sat on his hands and let them die, all the while ranting to his base that he would take out the opposition, God and Moses, in the upcoming election.

But God and Moses, the power duo, were kicking in his head at the polls as he found himself – a putative Egyptian deity– now flailing his arms and babbling pathetically about how they were involved in a massive conspiracy to defraud the public. He and only he, Pharaoh Raamses, had uncovered the ruse and would fight for the rights of the common man on the streets of Memphis, Pithom and Raamses, the town he had named for himself. Half of Egypt, sick, dying and exhausted, spat at him. The other half, sick, dying and exhausted, kept propping him up as their last chance to return to a golden age of power, just like in the good old days.

Ah, for the good old days -his good old days - when he was what those damn Israelites called melekh hadash, the new king. He had just completed developing a hundred new luxury pyramids, all of which he had financed in a lurid pyramid scheme. It had gone under the radar of the officials just long enough to allow him - a political neophyte whose handlers and whores had big dreams of royalty – to run successfully for national office. The ultimate elitist, Raamses figured out pretty quickly that if you target an outsider as the elite robber baron class you could get angry, marginalized Egyptians to believe in you and do whatever you told them.

That target was the Israelites.

Egypt's political and cultural life around that time had become a Blue Nile-White Nile divide. Blue Nilers were the more urbane progressive Egyptians in the big cities. They loved people like the Israelites, sometimes with a creepy kind of performative fawning, that helped them to reassure themselves that they were truly loving people, but they mostly had the genuine best interests of all of Egypt in mind. White Nilers lived on the farms, nursing conservative suspicions of people who didn't look and talk like "real" Egyptians. The foul undercurrent of some of their political waters was a rather unpleasant White Nile supremacism. They feared the onslaught of the hordes massed at Egypt's gates in Goshen province, hordes with names like Judah, Joseph, and Jacob. When they talked about making Egypt glorious again, many of them meant a glory whitened of all ethnic stains.

Raamses' first big rally after winning office was held at Imhotep's Columns, where a throng of MEGA swag wearing loyalists wildly cheered him on as he spewed and rambled.

"Now, I don't wanna say too openly what the real problem in today's Egypt is. You just never know when some Blue Nile libtard reporter will misquote you, and then you'll have to answer to the PC Police!"

(Derisive laughter from the crowd.)

"But folks, parts of this great nation have just gotten too CROWDED, dangerously crowded with other folks who want to grab the little that we have!

(The crowd boos.)

"So lemme ask you, folks. What should I do with all those crooked Goshen grandstanders crowding us good people out?"

"Lock 'em up! Lock 'em up! Lock 'em up!"

And lock them up he did, through decades of forced labor and human rights violations, none of which got even a peep of protest from the ruling White Nile politicos: they rationalized it all, but beneath all that was their one real rationale for doing nothing to stop Raamses:

You didn't mess with a god, especially one whom the people loved.

They sure did love him...and they were happy to support his hate campaign, especially since it made them happy to beat down people lower in Egypt than they were.

They sure did love him...and he hated them, but he adored their blind, butt-kissing, adulatory shrieks of praise, roaring their approval of him, calling his name...Pharaoh, Raamses, Pharaoh, Raamses, Pharaoh, Raamses..."

"Pharaoh...Raameses...sir? The Goshen Secretary of State is outside as you requested. Are you ready to speak with him?" His advisors were calling to him, pulling him from his reverie of manic, fragile self-love back into his ugly reality that he still refused to concede.

"Yes, of course," Raamses hoarsely barked, as he pulled himself close to the window of his palace bedroom.

Goshen was a weird, often toxic mix of Israelites and native old boy's club Egyptians, Blue Nilers and White Nilers, black skinned Nubians and white skinned folks. As the Blue Nile royal campaign team steamrolled through the towns, farms and cities, they won a significant majority of the populace desperate for a new Egyptian politics of compassion and accountability. For the first time in decades, Goshen - a White Nile bastion turned Blue and multicultural - threw its support behind the Blue Nile team. It was time for healing.

But the only healing Raamses was pursuing was the one spelled with two ee's. Besotted with manic rage, he kept pumping out the tired conspiratorial myth that his royal office had been stolen from him.

"You know, folks," he rasped irately to the faithful at his latest rally, "What is it that we actually won?"

"GOSHEN!" the crowd irately rasped back.

Yes, he would bring Goshen and its political operatives to heel: they would do a recount, a fraud investigation... something to prove that he won in Goshen, to show that he was still the chief.

The Goshen secretary of state stood below Raamses' window in the lovely sitting garden.

"Mr. Secretary, good to see you. Now, let me get to the point," Raamses growled. "I won in Goshen and I need for you to do me a favor: I need you to call the election for me. The fraud was everywhere in this contest, so find me 11,000 votes and let's get this done!"

"Pharaoh Raamses, sir. We have no credible evidence of fraud. Goshen goes to God and Moses. I'm sorry, sir."

"Mr. Secretary, this could mean trouble for you...legal trouble or worse, if you can't help me out," an agitated Raamses began to shout at him." "I don't want to have to call out all of my first-born elite guard to restore order!"

"Sir, you wouldn't be able to do that anyway. All of those first-born front line soldiers are dead. They died in the last plague pandemic. Did you not know that, sir?"

It was over, but Raamses, the narcissistic bowl of paranoid jelly, would never accept the fact that even a god didn't mess with God.

The newly freed Israelites prepared to stream out of Egypt, barely paying attention to their devastated Egyptian friends of the new order who begged them to stay and help to build the new Egypt.

"Look," one old man said to his neighbor, "We don't belong here anymore. And besides, you can rebuild Egypt yourselves. Someone quite so horrible as Raamses could never happen again. Trust me on that. I've seen it all. Good luck."

On the eve of the Exodus, some boys were playing in a field when they stumbled over a large stone with writing all over it. They lugged it to the middle of their street, near that same old man, their tribal elder, who was known to be able to read. As boys (and the happily well off) will do, they forgot about it.

Poring over the stone, the old man, who had indeed seen enough to last ten lifetimes, grimaced as he gradually deciphered the letters and words:

"That which has been will be in the future.

That which has occurred will occur again.

There is nothing new under the sun."

He shuddered at the warning and went back to packing for freedom.

This week we had a glimpse of what America can be

Rabbi Daniel Cohen

It is difficult to believe that we are only one week into the new year. So much has happened in the last week that it is hard to know where to begin.

This week we had a glimpse of what America can be.

I am not referring to the domestic terrorists who broke into the Capitol, terrorized countless people and murdered a member of the Capitol Police.

I'm not referring to the fact that some of those insurrectionists carried confederate flags or wore t-shirts with the most grotesque of antisemitic images and words imaginable.

And I am not referring to the fact that we saw, on camera, the difference between the way this week's insurgents were treated by law enforcement and the brutality with which Black Lives Matter demonstrators were met.

I am not even referring to the fact that, for almost two weeks, we will still have a President whose rhetoric has helped give rise to the growing epidemic of racism and hate and who, at a minimum, encouraged the violence that was unleashed this week.

No, I am not referring to any of that because for the past few years we have had much more than just a glimpse of such ugliness. It has become far too normalized.

What I am referring to is the fact that the State of Georgia will now be represented in the Senate by a 33-year-old Jew and a 51-year-old Black Baptist Preacher. (A preacher who plans to return to his pulpit on Sundays to preach to his community and then return to DC to serve ALL Americans.) And I am referring to the fact that the first First Woman and Woman of Color will be sworn in as Vice President of the United States of America.

And I am referring to the fact that the new Secretary of Transportation will be moving to Washington with his husband.

And I am referring to the fact that the incoming cabinet is diverse and filled with experts in their chosen fields.

And I am referring to the fact that the vast majority of this country watched the attempted coup this past Wednesday with horror. Because the vast majority of us wants a return to a government of the people, by the people and for the people…for ALL people.

This week showed us the ugliness that has metastasized at an alarming rate. But it also offered us a window into an America that might be. God willing, we will all continue to work together to ensure that it does.

Fear and Hope: Cleaning the Stains of Sedition from the Fabric of our Nation

Rabbi Jesse M. Olitzky

I finally fell asleep in the early hours of Wednesday morning, dozing off as election results from twenty-four hour news networks continued to flicker on the television mounted to the wall. Networks had declared Reverend Raphael Warnock the winner of his senate run-off election and Jon Ossoff had just taken a slight lead in his race for a senate seat. A state that once sat at the heart of white supremacy, where the Ku Klux Klan was reborn in Stone Mountain, a state that still celebrates that legacy with a monument, elected a black pastor serving Ebinezer Baptist Church, the spiritual home of Rev. Martin Luther King Jr., and a 33-year-old Jew.

Immediately, I thought of Chaney, Goodman, and Schwerner, the African-American man, and two Jewish men, who were murdered by the KKK in Mississippi during the Freedom Summer of 1964 while registering Black voters. Warnock referenced how his 82-year-old mother would pick cotton for white families and now, she was picking her son to be a United States Senator. In his victory speech, he referenced Rabbi Abraham Joshua Heschel saying that he prayed with his feet when he marched in Selma with Dr. King, and believed that Rabbi Heschel and Dr. King were smiling down on the Black preacher and Jewish millennial who were newly elected senators from Georgia. They were what the New South represented. A state that once celebrated segregation and discrimination, was represented by diversity and fighting for equality.

But within only a few hours, there was a pendulum swing of great extremes, from a historic moment that displayed the greatest of America to a moment in which we witnessed the worst of America. Following the charge by President Trump for his followers to march up Pennsylvania Avenue to the Capitol and "stop the steal," to prevent Congress from witnessing the counting of certified electoral college votes, a violent and armed mob of his supporters -- including the "Proud Boys" who Trump had only recently told to "Stand Back and Stand By" -- stormed the Capitol building for the first time since the War of 1812. A violent mob of domestic terrorists waving confederate flags and wearing MAGA hats, with shirts that read "Camp Auschwitz" and "6MWE," which chillingly stands for "six million wasn't enough," caused congressional representatives and senators to put on gas masks. Some were safely evacuated from side exits while many were hiding on lockdown in their offices with makeshift barricades of furniture being the only thing keeping their doors shut.

I wish I could say I was shocked. I was disturbed. I was angry. I was sad. But I was not shocked, since we know what happens when you pour gasoline on a fire. And that has what this President has been doing since he launched his campaign in 2015, stoking hatred and fear, siding with bigots and white supremacists. All of that came to a head on Wednesday afternoon, and America is forever changed. The scars of Trump's presidency will remain long after Joe Biden takes the oath of office. And the stain of this act of terror will remain stained on the fabric of our nation.

The Talmud[8] asks if it is permitted to sequester the coins of Jerusalem within the Temple, essentially hiding them. The Talmud says: "*U'va'u vah peritzim v'chileluha.*" Rabbeinu Gershom describes *Peritzim* as *Sonim*, enemies who fuel hate. The Talmud teaches that enemies who fuel hate will

---

enter the Temple and immediately desecrate it by their actions. Rabbinic literature recognizes that insurrection forever damages the sanctity of an idea, and the sanctity of a cause. The sacred halls of the Capitol are forever desecrated with broken glass, with the letters 'MURDER THE MEDIA" carved into wooden planks, and MAGA tagged unto the pillars. The Capitol has been desecrated and the Temple has been sieged, but this mob of terrorists did not only desecrate the Capitol. They desecrated democracy. And democracy is incredibly fragile.

Only hours after seeing the first Black senator and first Jewish senator from Georgia get elected, we saw the essence of racial disparity and brutality, by the way the National Guard who was called into action in riot gear during Black Lives Matter protests over the summer, teargassing peaceful protestors so the President could take a photo op, weren't called to stop an act of sedition, not when the group was all white, not when some law enforcement officers were even removing barricades and taking selfies with these terrorists.

The silence among some elected officials is deafening. The President telling the violent mob of his supporters to stop while still telling them he loves them and doubling down on his rigged election conspiracy theories is repulsive. And those politicians who only now call out this action, but not the President, after supporting the President, and propping him up for four-plus years, after equally fanning the flames of hate and conspiracy, are insulting our intelligence. As CNN's Jake Tapper put it:

> "'I decry violence; said the senator, while spilling gunpowder and gasoline all over the building and handing out matches."

When Moses is grown, he wanders out of Pharaoh's palace and sees a taskmaster beating a Hebrew slave. He sees the

141

direct result of his adoptive family's policies. He sees the direct result of his choice to be silent. The Torah tells us:

> *"V'yifen ko v'cho vayar ki ain Ish*. And then Moses turned this way and that way to see if there was any person around" (Ex. 2:12).

We make the assumption that he did so to ensure he wouldn't get caught before he stood up to the taskmaster. He looked around to make sure *ain ish*, that literally there was 'no man,' no person present. But we know that not to be the case. The Israelites were aware of Moses standing up to the taskmaster when they mentioned it the very next day. Because there were people around. They were everywhere. These were slaves in the middle of the desert. There was nowhere to hide. So what does it the mean that *ain ish*, that there was no man present? The sage Hillel teaches us:

> *"B'makom she'ain anashim, hishtadel lehiyot ish. In a place where there are no worthy people, strive to be a worthy person" (Avot 2:5).*

Moses saw people around, but no one was willing to step up and stop what was happening. And that was when he knew he had to. It came at quite the cost. He left the palace and a life of material wealth. He fled to Midian and became a shepherd. So I am unimpressed with a politician who edits their press release with a fine-tooth comb because they are more concerned with they own future political aspirations than they are with repudiating a tyrannical modern-day Pharaoh. I am encouraged by those who choose country over party, and integrity over Trump.

We need more people like Moses. The Torah tells us that no one ever again saw God *panim el panim*, face to face, like Moses did, but Moses was far from flawless. He too lost his cool as a leader and he was not able to enter the Promised Land. Still, I would settle for someone who is willing to step up -- even and especially -- when no one else has. It's easy to condemn when all around you is condemnation. It is courageous to do so when no one else is. It is courageous to look this way and that way, and to see the cowardice of colleagues who supposedly represent "we the people," who remain silent because they only represent themselves, and choose to speak up and call out an act of terrorism. When there are no worthy people, strive to be a worthy person.

This biblical narrative will lead to our eventual exodus from Egypt, *Yetziat Mitzrayim*, as Moses is tasked with taking the Israelites from slavery to freedom. *Mitzrayim* is often understood to mean *Mi-tzarim*, from narrow places. Moses is tasked with taking the Israelites – and humanity – out of a tyrannical fanaticism that is based on narrow-mindedness. On Wednesday, at the Capitol, we saw the worst of that narrow-mindedness. We saw the hatred and bigotry. We saw the violence and insurrection.

But, only hours earlier, we saw an example of light, with the election of someone who is unapologetically religious and progressive, one who uses his faith to unite and not divide, to preach love and justice, living Amos' prophetic vision that Dr. King could only dream about. Together, we will keep on spreading that same message. We will keep spreading a message of spiritual resistance. We will keep spreading a message of love. We will strive to be like Moses. And we will not let any one else's narrowness and hatred cause us to fear.

Rabbi Nachman of Bratzlav taught: "*Kol HaOlam Kulo, Gesher Tzar me'od*. The whole world is a narrow bridge." Throughout the world, we will confront the narrowness of hatred and bigotry, of fundamentalism and extremism. "*V'haIkar lo l'fached klal*. But the essence is that we shall not fear."

What will you commit yourself to today?

Rabbi Sydney Mintz

Today, (still)President Donald Trump told us: "our incredible journey is only just beginning." In case anyone thought that yesterday was an isolated incident or the lancing of a long festering boil, make no mistake, yesterday's events at the United States Capitol, literally the Temple of our Democracy, was one more instance of the cancer of hatred, racism, Antisemitism and ignorance that has been growing in this country for generations. Today we wake to the harsh reality that democracy is not and never has been a spectator sport. If we want a strong, vibrant and healthy democracy, each of us who still believes in the American Dream must dig in, speak up and out and get back to work. Voting every two years isn't going to bring us closer to what we dream about and what everyone in this country deserves-liberty and justice for all. Over 2000 years ago, the Babylonian Talmud taught us this: "*A ruler is not to be appointed unless the community is first consulted.* (Berachot 55a)"

I commit myself to working against this darkness and simultaneously seeing and recognizing the incredible work that went into giving this country the first African-American and first Jewish Senators from Georgia.

What will you commit yourself to today?

You might remember that in June of 2016 I helped to lead a nationwide Jews Against Trump protest before he became the Republican Nominee with Bend the Arc: A Jewish Partnership for Justice. I felt that it would begin a very traumatic and dark time in our history if he was elected

President. Through the past four years, the downward spiral away from justice has continued at an alarming pace even as those who seek a country based on liberty and justice for all have toiled ceaselessly to continue Bending the Arc of the moral universe towards justice. I kept asking the same question that so many also asked? What would it take for the world to wake up and see this for what it is? In this moment we see and are seen. We now understand the depth of the energy and commitment to dismantling justice and equity and replacing it with violence, hatred, racism, Antisemitism and depravity.

That downward spiral continues. The violence and insurrection at the US Capitol this week was not a culmination in anyway, it is one more wakeup call in the downward spiral. God asked Adam and Eve, "*Ayeka*-where are you?" in the Garden of Eden and we are being asked that same question today. Democracy is not Eden, but if we look away, if we give this moment a pass, we will all suffer.

Those Republicans who enabled and supported Trump should not be given a pass and those who actually voted for him a second time and have continued to support the blatant lies regarding the stolen election should not be forgotten in the chaos.

I shared three Photos with friends online from yesterday because I truly believe that this is not over, that the violence that was done and the mayhem that was allowed in DC will continue and in fact before the inauguration we will witness more violence and destruction as our democracy struggles to exist.

Two are from the Capitol, Camp Auschwitz, 6 million was not enough and one is the screenshot from my colleague's Shabbat service this morning that was zoom-bombed once again by Nazis and white supremacists.

I write to encourage you to stay vigilant and to be as proactive and communicative in supporting whatever campaigns or organizations you believe could use your help and support. Look out especially for your black and brown neighbors, the Queer community, Jews and Muslims, people who are underserved and economically and food insecure. Continue to face the truth when it comes to the pandemic and as my dear friend Dr. Larry Brilliant reminds us as we find ourselves in this dark tunnel of continuing deaths, wear your mask, stay six feet apart, wash your hands and don't breath other people's breath. It sounds like a repetitive mantra, and it is, almost 2 million deaths later.

When an unmasked (for Covid19) and unmasked (lacking any sense of fear around being identified as perpetrators in an insurrection) mob of thousands attack the center of our democracy, our shofar blasts: "Wake up now!" Let's get to work together, let's face the truth and not look away for a moment. I commit myself with you to continue the Holy Work of bringing the world to a better place, to shed light on the darkness and to believing that we will make a difference even as darkness continues to descend.

Justice, Truth, and Peace
Rabbi Ken Chasen

Dear friends,

Like you, I am exhausted, heartsick and stunned after what was surely the saddest day for American democracy in any of our lifetimes.

Whatever comes of the next thirteen days, today we witnessed the crumbling of our country's peaceful transfer of power. That is a stain that will never exit our personal or national memories.

A dear friend and rabbinic colleague of mine who serves a congregation in Washington, D.C. – and whose congregants work on Capitol Hill and survived today's unprecedented madness – spoke to his congregants tonight about how the peaceful transfer of power became sacred in the United States. He said, "George Washington gave up power not once but twice – at the end of the Revolutionary War, when he resigned his military commission and returned to Mount Vernon, and again at the end of his second term as president, when he refused entreaties to seek a third term. In doing this, he set a standard for American presidents. When told by the American artist Benjamin West that Washington was going to resign, King George III of England said, 'If he does that, he will be the greatest man in the world.' How far we have fallen…"

Indeed – today, regardless of one's partisan leanings, it is impossible to deny the historic smallness of the current President of the United States. His two-month assault on the truth about the presidential election has trampled upon democratic norm after democratic norm, and today was a direct result of his decision to conclude his term by fomenting insurrection, a decision unique in American history.

As law enforcement has re-stabilized the Capitol, Congress has resumed its business, and President-Elect Biden's Electoral College victory will soon be finalized, we have the opportunity to place this day's events into proper context. Our nation has proven durable against a previously unimaginable threat. While our democracy spent this day imperiled, it is spending this night in victory. When we go to bed, we must breathe in the blessing of living in a land capable of that victory.

And when we awaken in the morning, we must breathe out our vigilant defense of our country's soul. A historically small president remains in office for another thirteen days, and we can no longer claim to be surprised by any seditionist action he undertakes. We must let our national leaders know that we are watching and demand their protection from any further attacks on our democracy. Moreover, today's events laid bare once again deep fissures in our country regarding race, policing, the weaponizing of misinformation, and respect for the rule of law. We have enormous work to do in the years ahead – and our congregation, as always, will be committed to doing its part, in accordance with our Jewish tradition's moral call.

In the Jerusalem Talmud, Rabban Shimon ben Gamliel taught:

> "The world rests on three principles – on justice, on truth and on peace. And all three are intertwined. When justice is done, truth is served and peace ensues."

Let justice be done. Let truth be served. Let peace ensue.

To our Teachers, To our Parents

Rabbi Ravid Tilles

To our Early Childhood through 8th grade teachers:

My Dear Friends,

For the past number of hours, I have watched, in horror, the haunting images from the U.S. Capitol Building. Like so many of us, my range of emotion is running deep. Feelings of anger, fear, shame and disappointment are keeping me fixated on the news. As an adult, I know what these images mean and the weight that they carry. As an educator, guided always by my Jewish tradition, I wonder how we address this moment. I am sure that many of you, no matter your faith tradition, share my feelings of angst and uncertainty. So allow me to offer some guidance.

A moment like this should cause us to take stock of what values we share that are unequivocal. What are our highest ideals that cannot be politicized or denigrated but that must be passed to our students for the sake of that which we hold dear. The value of peaceful discourse and rhetoric. The values of civility and justice. The values of integrity and unity. The notion that words matter and should build up instead of tear down. So if you want to know if you are allowed to teach these values to our students, I would say that you MUST. At every turn, every day, without any fear of "political backlash" these are some of the values that cannot waiver.

So, as usual, we will ask that teachers use discretion on how we speak to students about the events of this afternoon, sticking to the facts while keeping in mind the political diversity of our school community. However, we will always support you in your fulfillment of our shared obligation - to teach the values that were attacked (and will survive) this afternoon.

May God bless us in our Holy work of teaching values to the future, and may God bless America.

With love and support,
Ravid

To our parents:

Dear Friends,

The traditional "Prayer for Our Country" elevates certain ideals that are cornerstones of our nation: peace and security, happiness and prosperity, justice and freedom. Today, the images of the raid on the U.S. Capitol was an assault on so much more than just bricks and mortar; it was an assault on our deepest values embodied by this building. I am sure that many of you, like me, have been terribly anguished by these images, watching in horror at what had felt unimaginable. And I am sure that, like me, many of your thoughts turned to your children and what these images will mean to them.

In response to this tragedy, our first step was to reach out to our teachers, who take their civic and religious duty to educate our children more seriously than I could possibly express. They are deciding whether and/or how to address this according to grade level. We have advised our teachers to be sensitive to the political diversity of our school community while being unequivocal about the need to uphold our deepest shared values and beliefs.

And now I turn to you, our parent community. We are certainly living in unprecedented times and have had to carefully weigh if and how to discuss this tragedy and other current events with our children. We support you in any way that we can.

My friends, I wish that we did not have to write notes like these so regularly. We pray for a day when the ideals of our Torah and this country - peace and security, happiness and prosperity, justice and freedom - may forever abide among us. Be well and stay safe.

The Desecration of the Temple of Our Democracy

Rabbi Daniel Greyber

with gratitude to, and continued prayers for the healing of, our rabbi, our teacher, Rabbi Steve Sager

A few years ago, I was honored with an invitation by our Congressman, G.K. Butterfield (D-NC), to attend a controversial speech by Israeli Prime Minister Benjamin Netanyahu to a joint session of Congress arguing against the Iran Nuclear Deal. My attendance was not an endorsement, but rather an honor and opportunity to be present for a momentous historical event. I still have the letter of invitation; I still have the ticket. I sat in Gallery 7, Row D, Seat 16. I remember looking at the seals of the Lawgivers — 23 marble relief sculptures that circle the upper walls of the gallery — and feeling pride, and a sense of home and ownership in seeing Moses and Maimonides alongside Jefferson and Justinian. I have a certificate commemorating my presence there, and a photograph with Congressman Butterfield, who honored me with his invitation.

I also want to tell you about the picture I don't have. Last year I attended the AIPAC convention in Washington DC and, on the Shabbat before, led a Conservative movement service at a Hartman Shabbaton before the convention. On Saturday night, I was lucky to join a special tour of the Capitol hosted for the Camp Ramah movement by Ramah alum, Congressman Ted Deutch (D-FL). We took pictures in the Rotunda and heard from Congressman Deutch about what it was like to work in the Capitol and then, at the end of the tour, he took us to the floor of the Senate chamber. Access to the chamber is quite restricted and, while we were permitted to sit at the desks, we were not permitted at the desk of the Vice President, the President of the Senate, and no pictures on the floor were permitted. I think a few people snapped some shots and were gently told to stop by the guard with us, but I didn't take any. That is the picture I don't have. There are some places so holy, photographs are not permitted.

The Capitol was described this week as the Temple of our democracy; the House and Senate chambers as the Holy of Holies. So when I saw the sickening photographs this week of a man swinging like a gorilla from the gallery balcony, or another one lounging in the chair of the President of the Senate, or another with his feet up in the office of Speaker Pelosi, I thought of the verse from Lamentations, " עַל הַר-צִיּוֹן שֶׁשָּׁמֵם, שׁוּעָלִים הִלְּכוּ-בוֹ, for the mountain of Zion which is desolate, foxes (or jackals) walk on it." It is the image of destruction, of calamity, of the temporary victory of evil; foxes prowling in holy space. The kinot (lamentations) of Tisha B'av declare: "Mount Zion has become desolate," Alas! Because we have placed an abomination on it. Alas! what has occurred to us."

I was supposed to be in Jerusalem this week for the winter session of the Hartman Rabbinic Leadership Initiative (RLI). Instead our cohort met on Zoom. We were trying to study theology on Wednesday when my 19-year-old son, Benjamin, came into my study and told me with a mixture of astonishment and fear in his eyes, "Abba, they are storming the Capitol." The next day, our cohort thought together about what Torah might teach us about this moment. Rabbi Mike Moskowitz shared a teaching with the group. Shemot, the Hebrew name of the book of Exodus that we start reading this week, is an acronym for "Shnayim Mikra v'Echad Targum.'. According to Berachot 8a:

אמר רב הונא בר יהודה אמר רבי אמי "לעולם ישלים אדם..."
פרשיותיו עם הצבור שנים מקרא ואחד תרגום
Rav Huna bar Yehuda says in the name of Rabbi Ammi: "one should always complete the reading of

one's weekly Torah portion with the congregation, twice from the *mikra* (i.e. <u>Torah</u>) and once from the <u>*Targum*</u>."[4]

From this we learn that Torah needs to be read twice, that while we may be tempted to look away, we must double-down. We must look again. In their translation and commentary on the Torah, Martin Buber and Franz Rosensweig demonstrated that the Torah contains *leitworts*, certain words that recur again and again in stories to signal the central theme of what's happening. The *leitwort* of the early chapters of the Exodus story is the verb "ראה" - to see.

Pharaoh tells the midwives, (Exodus 1:16) "וראיתן" when you <u>see</u> the birthstools, if it is a boy, kill it, if it is a girl, let it live." He tries to impose a way of seeing on the midwives. But the midwives refuse Pharaoh's way of seeing. Rabbi Jonathan Sacks (z"l) writes, "This is the first recorded instance in history of civil disobedience: refusing to obey an order, given by the most powerful man in the most powerful empire of the ancient world, simply because it was immoral, unethical, inhuman."

Moses' mom "<u>sees</u> her son, that he was good" (2:2) and acts to save him. Pharaoh's daughter opens the basket and <u>sees</u> a baby crying (2:6). Moses grows up and goes out and <u>sees</u> the suffering of his brethren (2:11), he <u>sees</u> an Egyptian hitting one of his kinsmen (2:11); he <u>sees</u> there is no man (2:12), nobody stepping forward to put an end to this, and he takes action. God, at the end of chapter 2, <u>sees</u> the children of Israel (2:25). At the burning bush, an angel makes itself <u>seen</u> in the burning bush (3:2), and Moses <u>sees</u> (3:2) and turns aside to <u>see</u> again (3:3). God <u>sees</u> (3:4) that Moses turns aside to <u>see</u> and, from there, the redemption begins to unfold.

This was a terrible week, a dark moment for America and a dark day for the Jewish people. Our instinct may be to turn away, to try and move forward from what happened. Yes, the forces of good, of law and justice, not violence and anarchy, won out as, at 3:30 the next morning, Congress certified the election of Joe Biden and Kamala Harris as our next President and Vice-President. But it is at our peril that we assume everything is okay. What we saw unfold at the Capitol this week must be studied and studied again.

In the Prayer for Our Country in Siddur Sim Shalom, we ask blessings ``for all who exercise just and rightful authority" and that God may "safeguard the ideals and free institutions which are the pride and glory of our country." We must see that President Trump has abused the authority of the Presidency and endangered those free institutions. We must see the racism inherent in the policing - or lack thereof - that took place on Wednesday, how violent white extremists were allowed to storm the Capitol building and then return home, leaving the police only later to track them down and hold them accountable for their crimes, while Black Lives Matter protesters this summer were met with tear gas and a massive show of force. We must see - and here I quote Republican NC Senator Richard Burr, a strong supporter of President Trump's agenda - how the repetition of "unfounded conspiracy theories" by President Trump has eroded the foundations of rational discourse that undergird the democratic process. We must see the terrible divisions that plague our country. We must fight our urge to demonize and cancel and unfriend each other. We must fight against social media algorithms designed to keep our attention by filling our feeds with people who agree with us. We must see that Facebook and other social media companies are trying to convince us that they are connecting us to the wider world when what they are really doing is, for the sake of massive profits, showing us a slice of the world that mirrors our own opinions. We must see hackers who are trying to pit us against each other, to fan flames and drive us further apart.

Not foxes, but people, entered the Temple of our democracy, its holy of holies, and ran wild this week. What do we do when a Temple has been defiled? In Maimonides' Laws of the Temple (5:10), he explains that, "[In] the northeastern [chamber], the Hasmoneans entombed the stones of the Altar which were defiled by the Greek kings." When the Greeks ran wild and defiled our Holy place, we did not just clean up everything and forget. We entombed the defiled stones. There was a room - the northeast chamber - where those stones were kept. A memory room. A room where people could go and look again.

How might we, as a country, or as a synagogue community, or just each of us as American Jews, create such a chamber? How might we entomb the defiled stones of this week? For myself, I'm adding a photo to the folder where I keep the memories of my invitation to the seat of our democracy. Perhaps we can talk with each other in the days and weeks to come to think about this question for our community and to help each of us figure out an answer for ourselves.

In a moment, we will stand and recite the Prayer for Our Country, and for Israel and for Peace. Some people have argued with me over the years - don't these prayers blur the boundary between religion and politics? We, of course, do not force any individual to say a prayer they do not want to say, but these prayers will remain part of our communal liturgy because since Jews were first exiled to Babylonia in the sixth century BCE, the prophet Jeremiah declared, "Seek the welfare of the city where I have sent you into exile, and pray to Adonai on its behalf, for in its welfare you will find your welfare." Religion that walls itself off from the world chokes and distorts itself; we are part of this world, we are part of this country; we dare not blind ourselves and look away. We recite a Prayer for our Country today not as a declaration of our country's or its leaders' rightness, but as an acknowledgement of its fragility and vulnerability. As Benjamin Franklin famously told a woman outside the

Constitutional Convention at Independence Hall in Philadelphia about the form of government being proposed inside, it is "a democracy, if you can keep it." Let us never take for granted the blessing of our democracy. May God give us the courage to see with the courageous eyes of Shifra and Puah, of Pharaoh's daughter, of Moses and of God, to look again at what unfolded this week, and to learn the lessons necessary for our democracy can stay strong, so we can keep it. Amen.

The Real Losers

Rabbi Adina Lewittes

וַיֹּאמֶר מֹשֶׁה אָסֻרָה־נָּא וְאֶרְאֶה אֶת־הַמַּרְאֶה
הַגָּדֹל הַזֶּה מַדּוּעַ לֹא־יִבְעַר הַסְּנֶה:

Moshe said, "I must turn aside to look at this great sight;
why doesn't the bush burn up?" (Shemot 3:3)

The Kotzker Rebbe urged us to study the narratives of
slavery and redemption as carefully as we study matters of
halakha/Jewish law for they, too, offer critical instructions
for the building of a just, free and peaceful world - the
mission of Judaism itself.

In the iconic scene of Moshe encountering a burning bush
we find one of the most urgent of these commands, one we
might describe as "Do Not Look Away."

A shrub that seemed impervious to fire catches Moshe's eye
and he turns to investigate. At that moment God initiates a
direct, plot-changing conversation with him that unfolds
over a whopping 40 verses - the longest running Divine-
human conversation in the Torah. Moshe's capacity to be
distracted from his daily tasks and intrigued by something
different, his willingness to inquire after something that
begged explanation, moves God to call out to him and
engage him in the sacred task of leading his people out of
slavery.

וַיַּרְא יְהוָה כִּי סָר לִרְאוֹת וַיִּקְרָא אֵלָיו אֱלֹהִים מִתּוֹךְ הַסְּנֶה וַיֹּאמֶר
מֹשֶׁה מֹשֶׁה וַיֹּאמֶר הִנֵּנִי:

When Hashem saw that he had turned aside to look,
Hashem called to him out of the bush: "Moses! Moses!"
He answered, "Here I am."

But what if the bush hadn't caught Moshe's eye or his interest? Would the story have ended differently? Only those who are primed to listen for the Universe's messages will hear them; only those who yearn for freedom will be liberated, and will liberate.

Just a few verses prior to this scene God hears the Israelites moaning under the burden of their oppression. Hearing their cries, God is moved to action.

The Sefat Emet explained that until their outcry the Israelites were so sunk in exile that they couldn't even feel it. Once they felt it and cried out, redemption began. The requirement for freedom is the awareness of your own slavery. To be in exile and not be aware of it – this is the lowest rung of human moral consciousness. As the Hasidic teaching says, it's not just the Israelites who were in exile, it was awareness itself that needed to be redeemed. Or, as Avivah Zornberg offers, it was the people's anguish that got God's attention because when we are dulled or desensitized to pain, we are unfit for redemption.

Like many, there is much that worries me, that angers me, that embarasses me about what's taking place in our country right now. But I feel especially afraid and ashamed of the message this moment is conveying to our children and grandchildren - to the next generation. We have failed to model an approach to community-building, to human decency, to social trust and to a principled embrace of diversity that reflects the best of what we can bring to our country, and, equally importantly, that would instill in the young the inspiration and dedication to bring their own best to their generation's leadership. Instead, we are bequeathing to them a culture of mistrust, dishonestly, partisanship, and fear which as we know leads to the worst and most dangerous of decisions. Among those will understandably be that devoting one's time, effort, resources and faith to the project of civic engagement and responsible government is not only a colossal waste, but even, as we've seen, a life-threatening enterprise.

What frightens me isn't just that to young people the solutions to our problems seem so elusive. What frightens me isn't just that, depleted and frustrated, the next generation may abdicate their responsibility to help heal humanity's pain. What frightens me is the risk that they will stop noticing; that they will stop paying attention; that they won't turn aside to look more deeply and ask מַדּוּעַ לֹא־יִבְעַר הַסְּנֶה -"what is this all about? What's going on here? Why doesn't the bush burn up?" And that they won't hear the voice that emerges, calling them to serve, to engage, to lead. And that they'll forget their line, "הִנֵּנִי/Hineni - I'm here."

Yes, we must declare that we are indeed very much awake; that we are concerned, we are paying attention, and we are committed to investigating - through study and action - the roots of our ills and their remedies. But in so doing we must be mindful of the fact that people are watching, namely, our future leaders. For their sake and as an expression of our love for them, we must turn to see with our own eyes, and inspire their younger eyes to never turn away.

Silence is Not an Option
Rabbi Rachel Kobrin

Dear Chevre,

I write to you this evening as a rabbi, as a mom, and as a human being. And as an American.

My morning began with joy. A black man and a Jew were elected in Georgia. Who would have thought it possible?

And then I watched Donald Trump's speech at his rally, and I listened to him as he riled up his followers. The appalling result was not a surprise.

I have spoken out about this man for years - sometimes dismaying congregants who have felt rabbis should be neutral and politics should not enter the synagogue. I have been criticized by those who feared the shul would lose money and by those who felt a sense of personal loss when Trump supporters chose to resign their memberships. I have also been called gutsy, passionate, and brave.

But let me share something with you - with my community - on this difficult evening: I did not speak out because I wanted to be brave. And I have hated losing congregants. I spoke out because I felt that I had no choice - because that is what Judaism demands of all of us. In the words of Elie Wiesel:

> "We must always take sides. Neutrality helps the oppressor, never the victim. Silence encourages the tormentor, never the tormented."

Silence is not an option.

Today we witnessed terrorism and white supremacy brought on by the terrifying man who has been leading our country for the past four years. Silence is still not an option. There is no room for neutrality.

We will move past this. The sun will rise tomorrow and we will breathe again. A new president will occupy the White House in two weeks. With a new leader, I pray that we can do the sacred work of promoting justice and peace. But we cannot become complacent and we cannot restrain our voices. We must demand that this seditionist, hateful behavior is called out for exactly what it is. We must work to remove white supremacy and fascism from our nation. We must once again hold compassion and truth as our highest ideals.

We will do this through activism. Through speaking. Through writing. And through prayer and song. We will not do this by stepping back, but rather by stepping forward. We will pursue justice - both when it is easy, and also when it is hard and when we are exhausted. This is the only way forward.

We will do it together. Not alone.

In the words of the psalmist: "You turned my mourning into dancing; You loosened my sackcloth and clothed me in joy." Psalm 30

May it be so. May we make it so.

Be the Ish!!

Rabbi Daniel Gropper

Watching the unbelievable footage from our nation's capital brought to mind a verse from this week's Torah portion,

> "Some time after that, when Moses had grown up, he went out to his kinsfolk and witnessed their labors. He saw an Egyptian beating a Hebrew, one of his kinsmen. Moses turned this way and that and, seeing no person (*ish*) about, he struck down the Egyptian."

Moses saw no one else stepping in to challenge the injustice he saw around him so he stepped up. This is the first example of him being an "*ish Tzedek* - a righteous person who stands for justice." We need a whole bunch of *tzedek* (Justice) and *mishpat* (righteousness - doing the right thing) right now.

Later, Rabbi Hillel said, "In a place where no one is acting like a human being (*ish*), be the human (*ish*)."

The same word, "*ish*," appears in multiple places. The lesson is clear. Be the *ish*, be the person, be the mensch, be the one.

Now, it certainly is possible that those who support the current administration could turn this verse upside down. I still see some of my conservative Facebook friends saying that the protesters had no choice because Congress wouldn't listen to them. Like Moses, they struck down the Egyptian after listening to a deluded president. Were they, in their movement's view, the *ish*?

To those people I say the following. The Talmudic sages were also uncomfortable with what Moses did. Among other reasons, they said that his act of murder disqualified him from entering the promised land. At the same time, Jewish law also speaks of the law of the Rodef - that one who sees another about to commit a crime (especially murder) is duty bound to step in, even to murder the pursuer. Sadly, Yigal Amir tried this as his defense for assassinating Yitzchak Rabin (the Israeli court - thankfully - quickly dismissed it). The fact remains, that one could look to the law of the *Rodef* to defend Moses. Moses saw a defenseless person being attacked. He stepped in and stopped the attack. He was within his rights to do so.

Of course, those who want to tear down the foundations of democracy on which our republic stands could try the same defense that Yigal Amir tried. They already are. It just doesn't work in the world that I inhabit.

As the phrase first proposed as a typing drill by instructor Charles E. Weller in 1918 succinctly says it, "This is the moment for all good people to come to the aid of their country."

#betheish.

Wholeness is a Moral Virtue
Rabbi Yael Ridberg

I have watched the unfolding of the events in Washington, DC and the Capitol building in disgust as the terrorizing crowds breached security teams and brazenly disrupted democracy in action. Americans broke into the hallowed halls of Congress incited by the President's lies and trampled the cherished norms of American values.

As the curfew gets underway in DC, I pray that calm and peace will prevail. Yet, as disgraceful as the events of today are, it bears remembering that just before the mob took over the Capitol and the news cycle, the Senate races in Georgia were called, and the first Black senator Rev. Raphael Warnock and Jewish senator Jon Ossoff won those contested seats. Their work together to change the course of history can serve as a counter narrative to the hateful actions that unfolded hours later.

The Psalmist offers, *"yehi shalom b'heilech, shalva b'armonotayich – may there be peace within your walls, tranquility in your palaces."*[9] Our tradition teaches that such wholeness is a moral virtue, that there is no room for seditious acts against the community. As Americans and as Jews we must remain vigilant that the values of citizenship and community stand firmly in opposition to the violent speech and actions that were unleashed today. Tonight, we pray for *shalom* and *shalva* – peace and quiet in the streets of Washington, DC and the preservation of our democracy.

---

[9] Ps. 122:7

The Pale Blue Dot

Rabbi Joel Mosbacher

In 1977, NASA launched The Voyager mission, with two twin spacecraft designed to cross into interstellar space and peer at our Solar System from the outside.[10]

Thirteen years later, on February 14, 1990, Voyager 1 snapped this photo of **Earth** from 3.7 billion miles away. It has come to be known as the "Pale Blue Dot," a term coined by astronomer and author Carl Sagan in his reflections on the photograph's significance, documented in his 1994 book of the same name.

The image shows a tiny speck all on its own, surrounded by nothing in the vast universe. In the photograph, Earth's apparent size is less than a pixel; the planet appears as a tiny dot against the vastness of space, among bands of sunlight reflected by the camera.

At the time it was taken, there was political turmoil here on Earth, as the former Soviet Union grappled with presidential elections and ultimate dissolution, ushering in a new world order and the end of the Cold War. The image of our lonely planet provided some much-needed perspective on our human condition.

Today, as political unrest, a financial crisis, and a global pandemic threaten our nation and our planet, the image, and the emotion it evokes, are still just as relevant.

In his 1994 book, Carl Sagan comments on what **he** sees as the great significance of the photograph, writing[11]:

---

[10] https://www.inverse.com/science/pale-blue-dot-puts-earth-in-perspective
[11] Pale Blue Dot: A Vision of the Human Future in Space, 1994.

"Look at that dot. That's here. That's home. That's us. On it, everyone you love, everyone you know, everyone you ever heard of, every human being who ever **was**, lived out their lives.

"The aggregate of our joy and suffering, thousands of confident religions, ideologies, and economic doctrines, every hunter and forager, every hero and coward, every creator and destroyer of civilization, every king and peasant, every young couple in love, every [parent], hopeful child, inventor and explorer, every teacher of morals, every corrupt politician, every "superstar," every "supreme leader," every saint and sinner in the history of our species lived there--on a mote of dust suspended in a sunbeam.

"The Earth is a very small stage in a vast cosmic arena," Sagan continues. "Think of the rivers of blood spilled by all those generals and emperors so that, in glory and triumph, they could become the momentary masters of a fraction of a dot.

"Think of the endless cruelties visited by the inhabitants of **one** corner of this pixel on the scarcely distinguishable inhabitants of some **other** corner, how frequent their misunderstandings, how eager they are to kill one another, how fervent their hatreds.

"Our posturings, our imagined self-importance, the delusion that we have some privileged position in the Universe, are challenged by this point of pale light....

"There is perhaps no better demonstration of the folly of human conceits," Sagan writes, "than this distant image of our tiny world."

Friends, for me, for so many of us, this has been a difficult week, filled with such a rush of emotions and concern for our corner of that pale blue dot. This feels like **another** moment of turmoil, like that moment 30 years ago when a spacecraft passing Neptune glanced back at us. The turbulent and surreal and yet somehow to be expected events in Washington, D.C. this past Wednesday are seared in my brain.

There was the moment when the President of the United States, at a rally, in tweets, and in a video from the White House, doubled and tripled down on his months-long incitement of violence.

And the moment when white insurrectionist terrorists, some armed, some wearing Antisemitic and white supremacist garb, stormed the Capitol building and **then**, when finally confronted four hours later by sufficient law enforcement, almost **all** walked freely back out of the building as if they had done nothing wrong.

And the moment when more than one quarter of the legislative branch of our government decided not to recognize the legitimately elected next President of the United States.

At each of these moments, my heart broke a little. I felt angry and scared and frustrated and helpless, and then angry and frustrated and scared, on a loop, like the loop of images that cable news kept cycling through every few minutes.

There were the images of our elected officials cowering in fear in the chambers of the House and Senate.

There was the image of four brave female congressional staffers grabbing and protecting the boxes holding the Electoral College certificates the lawmakers were in the middle of counting.

And there were the images of Senators and Congresspeople returning to their chambers to **finish** what they had **started**.

Photos can be **so** powerful, so emotionally evocative. A photo captures a moment in time-- freezing it for future generations to see, to remember, and to try to understand what that moment signified.

Candice Hansen, a planetary scientist at NASA who was part of the team behind the "pale blue dot" image, remembers that **one** of the messages that resonated with her at the time was how **alone** we are, that it's just **us** out here.

> "If we screw up our planet, we're screwing up ourselves," Hansen said. "We don't have another option, there's no plan b. We really need to take care of this world. Back then and now, it's kind of the same message."

This is a moment of choice, my friends, as helpless as we might feel. What will the photos from Wednesday say about **us** when people look at them in 2051, 30 years from now?

That story is not yet written. We begin to write it today.

There's a version of the story that history books recall, after they tell of what led up to that moment on Wednesday. The theme of **this** version goes like this: **that** was the day that American Democracy began its downward spiral. That was the day that **hatred** in our nation, hatred that long preceded the presidency of Donald Trump, was exposed **violently**, and was violently and intentionally turned against the core institutions of the United States, never to recede.

The prophet Jeremiah, living in his own troubled time in the 6th century BCE, asked the question, "Is there no balm in Gilead?[12]"

---

[12] Jeremiah 8:22

In **this** ending of the as yet **unwritten** story, the events of January 6, 2021, and the response of the people of America in the weeks, months and years to follow, made it clear that the answer to Jeremiah's questions was: **no**. There <u>was</u> no balm to the hate and rage that had been allowed to fester in that once great nation, that always **imperfect** but ever **striving** Union.

So goes **one** version of the story those images will tell our grandchildren and great grandchildren. In this telling, those photos show us the beginning of the **end**.

But there is **another** story that historians and philosophers and poets **might** write about what those pictures signify. It's a version that, to be honest, right this minute, feels about 3.7 billion miles from likely.

In this **other** version of the story, chroniclers will say that **that** was the moment that Americans realized that there was no plan b. **That** was the moment that Americans chose, as one, to choose a different path. **That** was the moment that Americans chose to see their commonalities as greater than their differences.

That was the moment that Americans began to see and hear and understand and rejoice in the capacity for human goodness, human kindness, and human decency in **all** of America's citizens.
And **that** was the moment that Americans decided to not **only decry**, but to work **relentlessly** to end dehumanization and violence, to stop standing idly by as our neighbors bled, to cease being silent in the face of wrongdoing and evil and injustice.

That was the moment, slowly, painstakingly, often with 2 steps backward to every step forward, that America and Americans began to live up to its creed, that **all** are created equal, that **all** are endowed by their Creator with certain unalienable rights.

That version of the story feels elusive at best right now. I know. It doesn't seem possible.

Right now, at this exact moment, it feels **safer** to assume that the 50 people who will begin to sit on **one** side of the aisle of the Senate on January 22 will **never** understand the 50 people who sit on the **other** side of the aisle.

It feels safer to bet that people **cannot** change-- that we **are** who we **are**. Some are built to **love**, and some are built to **hate**.

But we Jews are people of hope; we are inheritors of a faith tradition that audaciously asserts that the world as it is doesn't have to be this way.

My friends, this is not a kumbaya sermon. This is not a "why can't we all just get along?" sermon, either. This is not, I assure you, a "I'm sure everything will work out fine, don't worry," sermon.

Tonight I stand here, in fear and trembling. Perhaps you do too.

But I also stand here knowing that our grandkids, our great grandkids, and generations yet to be will look back on this moment in American history, at this moment in **human** history.

And **we** have to decide what we want them to **see** when **they**, like Voyager 1, look back as they leave our **orbit**, our **universe**.

And **here's** the thing: no **matter** how you **feel right now--** no matter how **I** feel, no matter how **we** as a **nation** feel, we

do have a **decision** to make about what story they will tell, what impressions those photos will make on **them** 30 years hence.

This pale blue dot is the place where every love and every hate, every moment of exaltation and every moment of human degradation has **ever** taken place.

About our Earth, Carl Sagan wrote,

> "To me, it underscores our responsibility to deal more kindly with one another, and to preserve and cherish the pale blue dot, the only home we've ever known."

Let's write **that** story-- the story when we realized **that**, and started to **act** like **that**, no matter how **long** it takes, no matter how long and arduous the journey to get there.

Because we **can**, if we **will**.

To close, I'd like to share a remarkable recording of a piece created by the composer Eric Whitacre, who, for years before the pandemic moved composers and cantors everywhere to create virtual choirs, has been bringing together singers from all over the world to make music. This piece is called *Sing Gently*, and it includes the voices and faces of an amazing 17,572 singers from 129 countries.

The lyrics are simple; they say:

> May we sing together, always.
> May our voice be soft.
> May our singing be music for others
> and may it keep others aloft.
>
> Sing gently, always.
> Sing gently as one.
>
> May we stand together, always.

May our voice be strong.
May we hear the singing and
May we always sing along.

This is not about Right and Left

Rabbi Aaron Melman

We are fortunate to live in a country that values democracy, peace, and equality. Our faith teaches us to respect others and to help those in need. We have every right, as Americans, to protest. We do not have the right to riot and cause chaos. I believe in democracy and I believe in the rule of law. We are seeing neither held up in high regard today. It is a sad day for this country I love so much. This is not about right and left, this is about right and wrong. At this most difficult time, I urge you to stay aware of current events happening in our nation.

The lawlessness that we observed today in Washington, DC is simply unacceptable and deplorable. What we are witnessing makes me angry, but more so makes me incredibly sad. I hope that the constitutionally mandated business of certifying the electoral votes can get back on track soon.

It is truly a shame that we are still hearing messages referring to an election stolen from the people. I pray for true leadership on both sides of the aisle moving forward. I anxiously await a peaceful transfer of power; with prayers for peace throughout our entire nation.

With Eyes Dimmed from Anger
Rabbi Sharon Kleinbaum

It's hard to come up with the words to respond to the events in DC. Armed rioters, incited by the President of the United States and the Republicans who refused to accept the outcome of this election, have breached the Capitol Building. These domestic terrorists overwhelmed the Washington DC Capitol police, are now roaming the building and have entered the Chambers of the Senate and House of Representatives.

It's too soon to know exactly how this will end. We knew that the days from the election on November third to the day of the Inauguration on January 20 would be difficult—and that once the election was confirmed over and over again, it was not impossible that violence would ensue. This is the way of authoritarians—to incite thugs to engage in violence and then say they "went too far." This is an attempted coup d'etat.

We will get through this together.

As we wait and watch in horror, we turn to the words of our ancient text of Tehilim/Psalms:

> My soul is utterly terrified, You Adonai, how long?
> Return, free my soul, protect me. Protect us for the sake of your name. I am worn out with my sighing, with my tears, I flood my bed. My eyes are dimmed with anger. Turn away from me all of you who do evil, Protect me Adonai, accept my prayer. (from Psalm 6)

וְנַפְשִׁי נִבְהֲלָה מְאֹד ואת יי עד מָתָי
שׁוּבָה יי חַלְּצָה נַפְשִׁי הוֹשִׁיעֵנִי לְמַעַן חַסְדֶּךָ
יָגַעְתִּי בְּאַנְחָתִי אַשְׂחֶה בְכָל לַיְלָה מִטָּתִי בְּדִמְעָתִי עַרְשִׂי אַמְסֶה
עָשְׁשָׁה מִכַּעַס עֵינִי עָתְקָה בְּכָל צוֹרְרָי

סוּרוּ מִמֶּנִּי כָּל פֹּעֲלֵי אָוֶן כִּי שָׁמַע יי קוֹל בִּכְיִי
שָׁמַע יי תְּחִנָּתִי יי תְּפִלָּתִי יִקָּח

I lift up my eyes to the mountain peaks
From where does my help come?
My help comes from You
Creator of heaven and earth.
Look and See!
You hold my foot firm on the ground
For You are constantly beside me.
My Guardian neither slumbers nor sleeps
But is always at my side to protest me.
The rays of the sun shall not harm me by day
Nor the light of the moom hurt me at night.
You will guard me from allthat is wrong
Protecting me from whatever my come.
You will safeguard my arrival
Protect my departure
Now and evermore. (Psalm 121)

אֶשָּׂא עֵינַי אֶל הֶהָרִים מֵאַיִן יָבֹא עֶזְרִי
עֶזְרִי מֵעִם יי עֹשֵׂה שָׁמַיִם וָאָרֶץ
אַל יִתֵּן לַמּוֹט רַגְלֶךָ אַל יָנוּם שֹׁמְרֶךָ
הִנֵּה לֹא יָנוּם וְלֹא יִישָׁן שׁוֹמֵר יִשְׂרָאֵל
יי שֹׁמְרֶךָ יי צִלְּךָ עַל יַד יְמִינֶךָ
יוֹמָם הַשֶּׁמֶשׁ לֹא יַכֶּכָּה וְיָרֵחַ בַּלָּיְלָה
יי יִשְׁמָרְךָ מִכָּל רָע יִשְׁמֹר אֶת נַפְשֶׁךָ
יי יִשְׁמָר צֵאתְךָ וּבוֹאֶךָ מֵעַתָּה וְעַד עוֹלָם

We pray for the health and safety of President-Elect Biden
and Vice President-Elect Harris, our senators, our
representatives and their staffs, the staffs of the Congress
and the law enforcement officers, and for the reporters and
the journalists.

We pray for a peaceful resolution and for our ability to come
together and reject violence and corruption and lies and
build a society based on justice, peace and truth.

If you're religious and supported President Trump

Rabbi Jeffrey K. Salkin

When he mocked the disabled reporter, did you laugh, or remain silent – or did you reflect on how such behavior violates biblical teachings about the disabled, and treating people like the image of God?

When he boasted that he could grab women by their private parts, did you smirk, or remain silent – or did you notice that such words violates religious teachings about respect for women and the proper expression of sexuality?

When he urged violence against reporters, did you cheer him on, or remain silent – or did you remember that religious traditions forbid gratuitous violence?

When he called for a ban on Muslims entering this country, did you rationalize that, or remain silent – or did you think about how such bans could theoretically turn against any religious group?

When he commented on the neo-Nazis marching in Charlottesville, and mentioned that there were "very good people' on both sides, did you nod in agreement, or remain silent – or did you ask yourself whether it is possible for neo-Nazis and Jew-haters to be "very good people?"

When he stood silently as his supporters called for the kidnapping of Michigan Governor Gretchen Whitmer, did you say that you could understand their frustration, or remain silent – or did you realize that "thou shalt not steal" also applies to stealing people?

When he lied numerous times a day, did you shrug it off, or remain silent – or did you wonder aloud about your religion's understanding of the meaning of truth?

When he characterized Mexicans as rapists, drug dealers, and animals, did you smile? Or, did you ask yourself how your religious tradition views the stranger and the immigrant?

When you knew about his and his father's real estate background – denying housing to African-Americans, did you say to yourself, "Well, that's business," or remain silent – or did you ask yourself about what your faith says about race?

When he denied climate change, defying science, did you say, "Well, that's his opinion…", or remain silent – or did you probe how religious teaching views our responsibilities to the earth?

When he used the Bible as a prop in front of a church in Washington, DC, and held it upside down, did you applaud his feigned religiosity – or, did you say: "Wait – that's my holy book…"?

When you heard that he was pro-life, did you embrace that stance without question? Or, did you somehow reason that it is hard to care about fetuses and not about real children in cages?

I could continue with this litany – or, as would be appropriate, chant it according to the haftarah (prophetic) melody.

But, I want to narrow my focus – away from that generalized thing called "religion," and focus on my own people, and those who proclaim my own faith.

President Trump won, according to the best estimates, somewhere between twenty and thirty per cent of the American Jewish vote. "Some of my best friends," relatives, and cherished congregants voted for him. I refuse to demonize them. They had their reasons for doing so, and I have long advocated that we need fruitful, heartfelt conversations about politics and values so that the various sides of the political chasm can truly hear each other.

But, if you are a Jew who cares about Judaism and its religious teachings, know that our faith is built on questions. You can't get out of the Passover Seder without encountering at least four of them.

So, I ask you:

When Trump said that he only wanted Jews and not Black people – to count his money, did you laugh? Or, did you frown?

When he pretended not to know who David Duke was and initially refused to refuse his support, was that acceptable? Or, did you somehow suspect that something was wrong?

When he retweeted an image of a Jewish star superimposed over a pile of cash, did you question it? Or, were you disturbed?

When you read Trump's quote about Jews: "A lot of you are in the real estate business because I know you very well. You're brutal killers, not nice people at all. But you have to vote for me, you have no choice" -- did you applaud? Or, did you begin to sweat?

When he told the Republican Jewish Coalition: "You're not gonna support me because I don't want your money. You want to control your politicians, that's fine" – did you smile knowingly? Or, did you say to yourself: "Wait a moment…"

When he addressed an audience of American Jews, and referred to Israel as "your country," did you agree? Or, did you say to yourself: "No, the United States is my country"?

When he constantly hemmed and hawed about the Proud Boys, the alt-right, and other anti-Semitic groups, did you skip over that, and find other reasons to continue your support? Or, did you start to worry?

When you watched what was unfolding on January 6, 2021, did you say: "Well, at least he moved the US Embassy to Jerusalem..." Or, did you ask yourself: "There is an affirmation of the embassy in Jerusalem, and there is an attack on the Capitol in Washington. Which of these acts is more important to me?"

When you watched what was unfolding on January 6, 2021, did you see the faces of the barbarians who attacked the Capitol? Did you realize that they were coming after our elected officials? Did you, at least once, ask yourself what Judaism thinks of government? (Clue: we say a prayer for the government in our services).

Did you see the gallows that was erected? Did you see the guy with the flag of the Confederacy? Did you notice the guy with the "Camp Auschwitz" T-shirt? Did you look at that crowd of miscreants, whose actions were truly, beyond measure, deplorable? Would you have felt at home in their midst?

Did you think about Germany in the 1930s? At least once?

Did you ask yourself: "Is this what my support of this man has finally wrought?"

All this time – for the past four years, and beyond: did you say nothing?

Did you ever read that little slice of Talmudic teaching: "Silence implies consent"?

If, all this time, you were silent – did you really mean for your silence to be consent?

What It Is to Be a Jew and a Patriot

Rabbi Ken Chasen

Shabbat is drawing near – and oh, do we need its restorative power... for the wounds from Wednesday's violent storming of the Capitol building will not be fading anytime soon. Not from the tattered fabric of our nation. And not from our own tattered and hurting souls, never to be quite the same again, after seeing images inside our nation's Capitol that we would dearly love to erase from our memories, but will now forever infect our vision of those hallowed halls of government.

On Wednesday night, I wrote to you all about my heartbreak – yours as well – in seeing the peaceful transfer of power, a hallmark of our national identity and pride, crumble before our very eyes. I expressed my heightened appreciation for living in a land that proved capable of withstanding the threat of violent insurrection – and also my renewed resolve, which I know you share, to be a part of demanding accountability, from the breached barricades all the way up to the White House. Each of us is reaching to reckon with our own role in surviving the peril of this moment and contributing to a better, safer, saner tomorrow.

This is what it is to be a Jew and a patriot – and let me be clear... being a Jew means being a patriot. That's not some new-agey invention to match message and moment. That's one of Judaism's absolute fundamentals, enshrined again and again in Jewish law. "*Dina d'malkhuta dina*," wrote our ancient sages more than twenty-five times in the Shulchan Arukh, Judaism's most authoritative legal code. It means: "*The law of the land in which we Jews live is the law.*" We are commanded as Jews to be good citizens. An important reminder after witnessing a mass abandonment of the responsibilities of citizenship unlike anything we'd ever even fathomed, much less seen.

And yet, we know the residue of the treasonous behavior we've seen this week will not vanish with the inauguration of a new president. The unhinged rage that came home to Washington this week has been brewing for years, and the road to recovering from it is long and fraught with danger. We may have endured the eruption for now, but the fissures remain. And we all know what they are, because we couldn't help but see them in all their ugliness on Wednesday.

At this moment when we are desperate for a vision in stepping upward as a nation, it's interesting that the Torah this week turned a page no less distinctly than our Congress did in certifying that the election is over. You see, this is the week when we begin this year's study of the second of the Torah's five books, the Book of Exodus. Yitzhak Abravanel, the 15th century giant of Spanish Jewish scholarship, saw the Torah as a roadmap for a complete spiritual journey, taken one book at a time.

Genesis, which we finished studying last week, is the personal aspect of the journey. It's a story of self and of family – our patriarchs and matriarchs, their tragedies and their triumphs. It's only as we begin the Torah's second book, Exodus, this week that the journey becomes national. This week, we meet Moses, and he begins to learn how to lead a people. And the people begin to learn how to be a collective. And they will fail sometimes. And wander. And suffer. They will even rebel and threaten to splinter apart at the seams. Sometimes, the book reads a lot like what we saw on Wednesday, in fact. But they will make it to Sinai – and they will be bound together by law, by Torah. They will step back from the precipice, and they will make it as a people. And we will be walking with them every step of the way, right as we are trying to complete that same part of the journey ourselves as Americans.

The Book of Exodus is about a people learning to take responsibility for itself and for each other. It's the very lesson this week's trauma has revealed we must learn as Americans. Are you looking for some vision for how to step upward as a nation? Come find it – right here with us.

Shabbat will be the perfect place to start walking with our ancestors through the Book of Exodus – and letting their roadmap point the way through our wilderness as a nation. Let us not be crushed by the heartbreaks of this week... let us instead be inspired by the opportunity and obligation to rise. Shabbat is where it all starts.

The DNA of the J-E-W
Rabbi David Spinrad

I have been accused of being "too political." I do not know what that means. I understand that when we gather, be it in physical or in digital space, sometimes we need sanctuary in our sanctuary. I get it. But week-after-week, month-after-month, year-after-year, I study our sacred texts and they never once counsel us to turn away from the brokenness or to ignore injustice in the world. Quite the opposite. We are the inheritors and I am a teacher of a tradition that this week reminds us that, long ago,

> "A new king arose over Egypt who did not know Joseph."

This king, this Pharaoh, set taskmasters over our ancestors to oppress them. But they then were and we are now schooled in the ways of the oppressed and skilled in the paths of the resilient. The more our ancestors were oppressed, the more they increased. The more they spread out. We survive. We even thrive.

When Pharaoh spoke to the Hebrew midwives, to Shiphrah, to Puah, telling them to kill the baby boys but to let the girls live, our Torah says these women summoned the unimaginable courage to reject Pharaoh's orders. This is our tradition. This is our Torah portion. This is the beginning of Exodus. These are the building blocks of our DNA. This is who we are.

When Pharaoh widened his decree, demanding the Hebrews throw their baby boys into the Nile to drown, one courageous woman, Yocheved, mother of Moses [and Aaron and Miriam] dared to resist. You know the story. Against the edict of a tyrant, she placed baby Moses into a basket, where he was discovered by Pharaoh's daughter and came to be raised in the palace. This is *"hashgacha pratit,"* divine providence. The unseen hand of God that touches all.

"And it came to pass, when Moses had grown up, that he went out among his brethren and he witnessed their labors. He saw an Egyptian beating a Hebrew, one of his brethren. He looked this way and that, and when he saw no person" challenging injustice, Moses stepped forward. In this moment, Moses for the first time acted as *"ish tzedek,"* a righteous person who stood for justice. The Rabbis later teach us,

> "In a place where no one is acting like a human being (an *ish*), be that human being."

Be that person. Be the one. Especially now. This is who we are. This is the DNA of the J-E-W.

You saw the events of Wednesday, January 6, 2021. The day began hopefully, if not with some trepidation for what lay ahead. The day began with the first Black person elected to represent the State of Georgia in the US Senate. And not just any Black person, but the senior pastor, the Reverend Dr. Raphael Warnock of Ebenezer Baptist Church, inheritor of the great legacy and tremendous responsibility that comes with occupying the pulpit that once belonged to the Reverend Dr. Martin Luther King, Jr., may the memory of the righteous be ever for a blessing. The day continued with the news that the first Jew, Jon Ossoff, had been elected to represent the State of Georgia in the US Senate. It is significant any time a Jew achieves this recognition, but it is made doubly so when we remind ourselves that at The Temple in Atlanta, where Jon Ossoff became a bar mitzvah, there hangs a photograph of Leo Frank, a Jew, an innocent man who was framed and hanged by an angry mob in 1913.

But instead of celebrating a day of firsts, we witnessed not just another "here we go again" but the terrifying-yet-logical next step in the arc of a wannabe authoritarian, a would-be tyrant's assault on democracy and on the three things our Rabbis teach us upon which the delicate balance of the world depends: our world balances on truth. It balances on justice. And it balances on peace.

Our world is way out of balance. And for the past four years President Donald J. Trump, *yimakh shemo*, has done all he can to knock our world off of its axis. Of all of the powerful feelings I have tonight, surprise at the attempted insurrection, disbelief at the failed the *coup d'etat*, confusion over the seditious acts are not what I am feeling.

This tyrant was in ascent for years. But because of the seductive nature of position, privilege, and power and out of fear of losing them, those who could have stood up to him did not when they could have and those who have and did, did it too late. After years of an assault on truth, peace, and justice, and after weeks or urging his supporters to descend on DC to stop what he insisted was the stealing of the election, the President stood before his mob and lied that he had won the election. He said, "We are going to have to fight much harder." He told them to march on Congress to "save our democracy."

The rioters took Trump at his word. You know the story. You've seen the images.

If I am being too political for bringing this to this sacred hour, if tonight "sanctuary" means not an escape from reality but instead getting real about this moment, so be it. I work for you, but I serve God. And I have a duty to honor the memory of my Holocaust survivor grandparents, the memory of my mother, who was born in a displaced persons camp in Germany after the war, Gal's grandmother, who survived Auschwitz, and the responsibility of raising children, one of whom is a young woman and the other who is a Jewish and Black boy. Out of honor and respect for them,

I will never get over seeing the Confederate flag fly in Congress. I will never forget seeing the "Camp Auschwitz" sweatshirt on one rioter or the "6MWE," meaning "six million wasn't enough" shirt on a Proud Boy and I will never forgive President Trump, who encouraged the Proud Boys to "stand back and stand by." And I will not forget or forgive that he then took to Twitter and told these traitors, "We love you, you're very special."

But while the Jewish people have our mourning rites and our days of lamentations, we are discouraged from pessimism. In fact, one of the Jewish people's great strengths is we are a hopeful people. Later in our Torah portion, Moses meets God for the first time, at the Burning Bush. Tasked with going to the Hebrew slaves to tell them that a great change is going to come, that God was going to take them out from slavery on eagles' wings, Moses told God that the enslaved were not going to believe him. He said, "Tell me you name," so I can tell them who You are, God. God responded, "*Ehyeh asher ehyeh*." I will be that which I am becoming. The subtext is God isn't done becoming God.

I want to go one step further. Although these days are dark, God lives through us. God calls us. God can't do it without us. God needs us now. Do not despair. This is not the end. We will turn this page. A new chapter will begin. And when it does, let us have the courage to speak truth to power and to remember the DNA of the J-E-W. Let us be like the midwives, Shiphrah and Puah, who rejected Pharaoh's deathly command. Let us be like Yocheved, who dared to resist and put her baby Moses into the basket. But most of us all, let us be our very best selves, courageous in our determination to co-create with God and with each other a world of truth, justice, and peace.

Amen.

This is a Reckoning

Rabbi David Lerner

This is a reckoning.

On Wednesday, we witnessed the lowest moment in American history since slavery, the secession during the Civil War, and the Jim Crow laws and segregation.

The images are seared in our minds forever. An angry mob of rioters storming the capitol incited by the president of the United States.

The president of the United States and other elected officials and their enablers encouraging people to engage in domestic terrorism, an armed insurrection.

> And they did.
> I wish I could say I was surprised.
> I am not.
> I am disgusted.
> I am saddened.
> I am ashamed.

Our democracy has been sullied and violated in a way that it has not been since 1865.

Democracies are fragile; as Ben Franklin said, "It's a republic, if you can keep it."

If you can keep it.
If you can only keep it.
Can we keep it?
I honestly don't know any more.

And we have shown that we have been far too complacent.

Too many of us have said Trump is just noise.
Or this one: "But, he is standing up for Israel."
Or: "he is helping our economy."
Or: "look at the stock market."

I have listened to his supporters.

I wish I could say otherwise, but there is no justification for him. We cannot "stand back and stand by" as he told the Proud Boys in the first presidential debate.

I cannot stand idly by.

"Lo ta'amod al dam reiakha - do not stand idly by" - when blood is spilled and blood has been spilled.

Five people died on Wednesday. A woman who bought the lies spread by ReTrumplicans. A police officer. Three others who died of medical incidents.

56 police officers were injured.

This was not an accident.

This was caused by an act of sedition by Donald Trump and his son Donald Jr., Rudy Guiliani and others who spoke at the rally that sent thousands to attack the capitol.

Our members of Congress - from both parties - crouched on the ground, fearing for their lives.

The images are searing: Congresswoman Susan Wild lying flat on her back in the House chamber in terror while a former Army Ranger, Representative Jason Crow tries to calm and protect her.

The members of Congress running for their lives from armed insurrectionists.

The image of the officers in the Capitol with guns drawn to the doors to protect those inside. The president turning on his vice-president sending his "troops" to attack and stop the certification of an election.

Which is when these traitors started yelling: "Where's Pence, where's Pence."

The endless lies that have been promulgated ceaselessly on Fox News, NewsMax, Parler, and by the Sinclair Media Group.

This led to tens of millions of the 74 million people who voted for this narcissistic psychopath to believe the election was stolen and thus, the only option for them was violence.

This is a reckoning.
This is a reckoning.

But it is not just about the unhinged egomaniac. That's far too simplistic. That's far too easy. This is not just about one man.

This is about a broken system with far-reaching flaws. This is about a country that has a broken media that spreads lies worse than 1984.

This is about a country that shoots black men for standing on street corners and beats and shoots them in peaceful protests, but allows white supremacists to run willy-nilly through the halls of Congress, desecrating hallowed ground.

I have been to Congress, I have visited our elected officials there; it is an honor to lobby them, to speak with them - to engage in democracy asking them for support for Israel, asking them to stop gun violence. I have seen the hard work of the government.

But now, we saw 139 members of the Republican party join a farce - a lie, encouraging the overturning of an election. They had no right and NO basis to do this.

And some Republicans called them out for this terrible act which encouraged all this violence.

Three Republican governors including ours have called for President Trump to resign.

This is about a broken political party.

This is about Senator Hawley of Missouri who has blood on his hands according to his own hometown newspaper. His raising his fists to the terrorists, encouraging them to violence.

This is about Senator Cruz who supported and ran the president's delusional election claims.

> This is about white supremacy run amok.
> This is about growing anti-Semitism.

What did we see on Wednesday?

> The man wearing the Camp Auschwitz sweatshirt.
> On the back it said "Staff."
> The Neo-Nazis.
> The 6MWE T-shirts.

What does that stand for? 6 million wasn't enough. 6 million wasn't enough!!! This is the basket of despicable deplorables the president mobilized.

What have we seen since Trump was elected?

He called those who chanted "Jews will not replace us" "very fine people" after the hate rally in Charlottesville back in 2017, then he engaged in frequent anti-Semitic tropes. He encouraged violence which led to the mass shooting of the shul in Pittsburgh since that synagogue supported HIAS, which is a Jewish organization that helps immigrants which the president opposed.

And these anti-Semitic tropes have been ignored because, well, he's so good for Israel - he moved the embassy.

Come on.

If you play with fire, you're going to get burned.

Where was the leadership over the last four years calling out the non-stop hate?

> I have been told, "Oh, those are just tweets."
> Really, just tweets.
> Words, words lead to violence.
> *Words kill.*

*   *   *

Now today, I could stand before you or rather sit and tell you this is a sad day for America, but new leadership is coming and better days are ahead. I could give an innocuous sermon and not get too "political."

> I could say this is a bad time. There are people saying negative things on both sides of the aisle.
> But, I can't.
> I can't do it.
> I won't do it.

I have listened to different views. I have taken them in. I have meditated and thought about what's going on.

> And this is not the time for that.
> That is simply wrong.
> My friends, this is a reckoning.

For all of Trump's apologists. For over half the Republican caucus in the House who still voted for the lie that the election was not fair.

> This is a reckoning.

For those who arrest the black lives matter protestors, but did not arrest those who committed treason on Wednesday, this is a reckoning.

> Why were so few arrested?
> Because this angry mob was white.
> Again, we must come back to the racism deeply embedded in our country.
> The Confederate flags.

This is a broken country. A country that cannot wear masks to stop a pandemic since its leader didn't think it looked good on him.

A country where there were other armed rallies all around the country like the pro-Trump protestors who broke through the gate at Governor Inslee's mansion in Washington State.

A country where men with long guns roamed around capitals across the country, a country filled with right-wing hate groups who want no gun control and move freely with their weapons intimidating the rest of us.

A country which is trying to undermine the new administration before it even takes office.

A country filled with right-wing hate groups who posted on social media what they were going to do and no one prepared for it!

A country which allowed these criminals to commit crimes and then go home freely.

A country where some Republicans are lying about who committed these acts of sedition, claiming they were not Trump supporters but Antifa.

*   *   *

It's important to note that even the Wall St. Journal has finally awakened to the truth, asking Trump to resign.

This is a reckoning.

As Tom Paine told the colonists in Common Sense in January 1776, in a monarchy, "the king is the law, but in a free republic, the law is king."

This is a man who said he could "stand in the middle of Fifth Avenue and shoot somebody" and not lose any voters.
This is what he said, what he believes.

What does the president think about the storming of the Capitol endangering people's lives? He enjoyed it. He liked seeing his name on large flags. That's what ego-maniacs do.

What does he think about the domestic terrorists? He said: "We love you. You are very special."

This is a time for reckoning.

*   *   *

This president would not agree to a peaceful transfer of power.

Why?

> Because he does not want to.
> Because his only objective is to retain power.
> Because he cares only about himself, his money, and his power.

Most presidents don't want to give up their power, but they have and they do because it's how democracy works.

> Now his cabinet, his aides are resigning.
> Come on - too late.

Where were you before when we needed moral leadership?

Where were you when the president abdicated his leadership, letting more than 300,000 people die unnecessarily of Covid?

Where were you when we needed someone to protect the children - two-year olds separated from their parents at the border?

Where were you when the president made his disgraceful phone call to the Ukraininan president like a mobster?

Where were you when Muslims were being banned from our country?

Where were you when the president ridiculed people with disabilities?

Where were you when the president fomented hate?

Where were you when the president lied every day?

Where were you when the president was impeached?

Where were you then?

This is a reckoning.

*   *   *

Our Torah presents us with a different image of leadership. Moshe is a shepherd, a leader who is filled with care and concern for others, for his flock. He is a person of compassion. A person with integrity. He cares for his entire flock, not just some of them.

After God hears the suffering of the enslaved Israelites, the spotlight turns to Moshe, who is driving his flock into the midbar, the wilderness.

Why?

Rashi says because Moshe was a moral person and wanted to make sure that his flocks would not graze on someone else's land.

Sforno, a later Medieval commentator, says Moshe went to meditate.

Rabbi Kushner in our Etz Hayim Humash points us to the wonderful midrash which explains that he went into the wilderness to rescue one lamb that ran away; God realizes this is a man of compassion.

What is a moral leader?
A person of honesty and integrity.

A person who meditates, searching for God's presence, a mystic who can be introspective.
A person of compassion.

But Moshe is more than that. According to another midrash, he was not the first one to walk by the burning bush; others did before him, but they did not notice it. Moshe stopped and noticed it.

And then, and only then, did God call him, did God speak to him from the bush.

A leader is someone who notices, who looks around and appreciates the world around her.

And how does Moshe respond to God's call: with the greatest response in human history: *Hineni* - here I am!

I am ready to be a moral leader.

I am ready to stand in the breach.

I am ready to call out injustice.

I am not afraid to call out horrible, seditious acts.

A moral leader speaks out against racism, misogyny, bigotry, hatred, anti-Semitism, violence, White Supremacy, and speaks for those on the margins, the poor, those who have Covid, those who are disabled, those who are need of homes, those who are out of work, those who are hungry, those who might be evicted.

A leader says: *Hineni*: Here I am - I am ready to serve others, not myself.

And finally, a leader is reluctant to lead, a leader does not thrust themselves into the spotlight. When Moses is asked by God to go to Pharaoh, he says: Mi Anokhi - Who am I that I should go to Pharaoh and free the Israelites from Egypt?" (Ex 3:11)

Our ancient prophets, our great moral leaders from Moses to Jeremiah were reluctant to lead as they were filled with humility, not egocentrism.

God chooses the humble to lead, not the arrogant.

That is the moral leadership our Torah calls for and that is the moral leadership that we need.

And while this is a reckoning, even amidst the violence and chaos, I saw the glimmers of that leadership.

On Wednesday night, I stayed up with the Members of Congress. I watched as they reconvened in the holy ground of Congress which had been defiled just hours before. I thought of the Holy Temple in Jerusalem when the Maccabees regained control after the idolaters were removed.

I thought of when I lived in Israel and people wanted to go to the cafes that had just been bombed by terrorists in order not to give them any kind of victory.

I thought of those including me who wanted to run the Boston Marathon after the Marathon Bombing.

Our representatives did not let domestic terrorists stop the certification of the presidential election, even though the president and his insurrectionists and ReTrumplicans tried to overturn it, and they succeeded in delaying it. Even with the windows and doors smashed in, they returned to their chambers to vote.

I never thought the most boring and rudimentary counting of the electoral college would be so moving...

I had to watch until the end and finally, at 3:39 AM the election was certified, every electoral college vote was counted.

Our representatives showed up, did their jobs, though those who voted with the president will have to answer for their actions. They will have to answer for their complicity.

This is a reckoning for them and their constituents.

*   *   *

So, my friends, this is a moment we will never forget. This is one of the lowest moments in American history.

This is a reckoning.

But the Jewish way is to hold onto hope. Hold your children close, your grandchildren close, your loved ones close, your friends close, your community close, your country close.

Know that there is another model:

> - a model of moral leadership that Moshe
> exemplifies in our Torah.
> - a model of integrity, compassion, and humility.
> - a different model.

Let this reckoning bring about that moral leadership and let us all say: *Amen.*

We Are Not Alone
Rabbi Asher Lopatin

Friends, we have just experienced trauma - horrific trauma to our country, our democracy and to ourselves as Jews. The combination of antisemitic themes and vicious hatred, and incitement by our President and many others, left us broken and sad, but, I hope, with a renewed sense of purpose and mission as a Jewish community that cares about laws, about our country and about never again letting mobs rule.

In Egypt, in this week's parsha, Moshe sees oppression and lawlessness and looks in all directions, and sees nobody. Thank God, we look around and we see allies, friends and millions who share our love for America as a democracy and as a fair and honest nation.

I hope you take this difficult time as an opportunity to perhaps step out in the cold more than usual, come to a Friday night service and sing, or to Shabbat morning and hear this incredible Parsha, or just walk in the street and say Shabbat shalom or hello to people and make them smile and wave. Let us make sure that when we look around for comfort, hope, and safety, that we see each other and we do not feel like Moshe, that we are alone.

You are not alone! Join with those around you to show your own strength and hope and let others feel confident and comforted to stand alongside you.

May this Shabbat bring peace and comfort and a vision for a better future.

God bless America!
Shabbat shalom!

Contributors

Rabbi Rachel Ain is the Rabbi of Sutton Place Synagogue. Rabbi Ain served as the Senior Director for National Young Leadership at the Jewish Federations of North America, and the Senior Rabbi of Congregation Beth Sholom-Chevra Shas.

Rabbi Adam Baldachin is the rabbi of Shaarei Tikvah in Scarsdale, NY.

Rabbi Jonathan Blake is senior rabbi of Westchester Reform Temple in Scarsdale, New York.

Rabbi Sharon Brous is the senior and founding rabbi of IKAR in Los Angeles.

Rabbi Ken Chasen is Senior Rabbi of Leo Baeck Temple in Los Angeles. An outspoken advocate for social justice, Rabbi Chasen's writings have appeared in numerous books and publications, including the Los Angeles Times, The Forward, Variety, Thrive Global, and The Jewish Journal, among many others. In addition, he is a member of the adjunct faculty of the Hebrew Union College – Jewish Institute of Religion, serves as National Co-Chair for T'ruah: The Rabbinic Call for Human Rights, is an appointee to Los Angeles Mayor Eric Garcetti's Interfaith Leadership Collective, and is a prominent Jewish composer whose works are regularly heard in synagogues and schools around the world. He is married to Allison Lee, the Chief Development Officer of TIME'S UP, and they are the parents of three children.

Rabbi Daniel Cohen is a native of New Jersey. He came to Temple Sharey Tefilo-Israel in South Orange, NJ in 1992 while still a student at the Hebrew Union College-Jewish Institute of Religion (HUC-JIR) in New York. Ordained by HUC-JIR in 1993, he remained at TSTI as Assistant, then Associate Rabbi and has served as the congregation's Senior Rabbi since 1999. A graduate of Duke University, Rabbi Cohen holds a Masters of Arts in Hebrew Letters and Rabbinic Ordination from HUC-JIR. He earned a DMin in Pastoral Counseling from HUC-JIR and the Post Graduate Center for Mental Health in 2001. Rabbi Cohen lives in South Orange with his wife Raina Goldberg and their goldendoodle Nava.

Rabbi Elliot Cosgrove is the rabbi of the Park Avenue Synagogue in Manhattan.

Rabbi Gary S. Creditor is Rabbi Emeritus of Temple Beth El in Richmond, VA. His most recent book is "Praying for Our Country."

Rabbi Menachem Creditor is the Pearl and Ira Meyer Scholar in Residence of UJA-Federation New York and the founder of Rabbis Against Gun Violence. His 24 books and 6 albums of original music include the global anthem "Olam Chesed Yibaneh" and the anthologies "When We Turned Within" and "None Shall Make Them Afraid."

Rabbi Noah Zvi Farkas serves at Valley Beth Shalom, the largest Jewish congregation in the San Fernando Valley. He was ordained at the Jewish Theological Seminary of America in 2008, where he won numerous academic prizes in the areas of Jewish Philosophy and Talmud. He is also a Lecturer at the American Jewish University.

Rabbi Aviva Fellman is rabbi of Congregation Beth Israel in Worcester, MA.

Rabbi Ron Fish is the spiritual leader and Senior Rabbi of Temple Israel in Sharon, MA. He has served congregations in Norwalk and West Hartford, CT and is a member of the Massachusetts Board of Rabbis executive committee. He is a consistent and leading voice for pluralism, human dignity and Jewish unity in the face of difference.

Rabbi Eli Garfinkel grew up in Indiana, received a B.A. from Indiana University in 1993 and rabbinical ordination from the Jewish Theological Seminary of America in 1999. In 2005, he became the spiritual leader of Temple Beth El in Somerset, New Jersey, where he started an annual Jewish film festival, organized communal Passover seders, and taught popular adult education courses. He is a past president of the New Jersey Rabbinical Assembly. He is the author of the (forthcoming) JPS Jewish Heritage Torah Commentary. He lives with his wife, Naomi, and their twins, Sari and Josh.

Rabbi Lisa Gelber is rabbi, mother, marathon runner, spiritual director, breast cancer survivor and PELOTON enthusiast. She serves as Advisory Committee member of BFOR: The BRCA Founder Outreach Study (BFORStudy.com) and speaks nationwide about domestic violence in faith community. Lisa sits on the Executive Council of the Rabbinical Assembly and the NYBR Board of Governors. She was featured in the Emmy Nominated Documentary ALL OF THE ABOVE: Single, Clergy, Mother. Lisa fills her days as spiritual leader of Congregation Habonim on the Upper West Side of Manhattan where she lives with her daughter and Torah muse, Zahara.

Rabbi Adir Glick is rabbi at Temple Har Zion in River Forest, IL in the Western suburbs of Chicago. He is involved in interfaith initiatives throughout Chicago and teaches Jewish meditation to groups of all ages. Prior to entering rabbinical school, Rabbi Glick worked as a journalist for the Jerusalem Post and the Jerusalem Report magazine. He received degrees in Creative Writing and Journalism from Concordia University in Montreal. He also spent a year in Nepal working for the Israeli humanitarian organization, Tevel b'Tzedek. He was ordained in 2015 by the Ziegler School of Rabbinic Studies of American Jewish University in Los Angeles. He is married to Rachel and has two children, Shalva and Adiv.

Rabbi Daniel Greyber is rabbi at Beth El Synagogue in Durham, North Carolina, author of Faith Unravels: A Rabbi's Struggle with Grief and God, and currently in cohort VII of the Rabbinic

Leadership Initiative of the Shalom Hartman Institute in Jerusalem. Greyber served as Team USA Rabbi at the 19th and 20th World Maccabiah Games in Israel. Formerly a Jerusalem Fellow at the Mandel Leadership Institute, a faculty member at the Ziegler School of Rabbinic Studies in Los Angeles, and the Executive Director of Camp Ramah in California, Rabbi Greyber's articles have been featured in a wide range of Jewish publications.

Rabbi Daniel Gropper is the spiritual leader of Community Synagogue of Rye, past president of the Westchester Board of Rabbis and serves as secretary to the board of Repair the World.

Rabbi Jen Gubitz lives in Boston and pursues a rabbinate committed to elevating Jewish wisdom's capacity to speak to our human condition.

Rabbi Nicole Guzik is a rabbi at Sinai Temple in Los Angeles, CA. Among her pastoral responsibilities, Rabbi Guzik focuses on Israel programming, educational support for children with special needs, women's programming and creating community for families with young children. She is pursuing her Masters in Marriage and Family Therapy in order to bring awareness to mental health in the Jewish community. Rabbi Guzik is married to Rabbi Erez Sherman. They are the proud parents of Annie, Zachary and Henry.

Rabbi Eytan Hammerman is rabbi of the Jewish Community Center of Harrison, NY.

Rabbi Sharon Kleinbaum serves as spiritual leader of Congregation Beit Simchat Torah. For many years Rabbi Kleinbaum has been ranked by Newsweek among the 50 most influential rabbis in America.

Rabbi Rachel Kobrin is the spirtual leader of Congregation Rodef Shalom in Denver, CO. She is a Clal Rabbis Without Borders Fellow and a member of the Faith 2020 Advisory Group, which partnered with Believers for Biden in working to elect Joe Biden and Kamala Harris.

Rabbi Marc Labowitz is a teacher, lecturer and award-winning composer serving as the Rabbi of Temple Adath Or, in South Florida since 2002. Rabbi Labowitz's deepest spiritual practice is to foster a world in which Freedom, Acceptance and Love are the essence of all paths. He endeavors to do this by creating a wise, warm, vibrant, caring community, based on Judaism, and the teachings of our Sages.

For the past seventeen years, **Rabbi David Lerner** has served as the spiritual leader of Temple Emunah in historic Lexington, MA, where he is now the senior rabbi. A graduate of Columbia College and ordained by the Jewish Theological Seminary where he was a Wexner Graduate Fellow, Rabbi Lerner brings to his community a unique blend of warmth, outreach, energetic teaching, intellectual rigor and caring for all ages. Rabbi Lerner has served as President of the Massachusetts Board of Rabbis and the Lexington Interfaith Clergy Association. He is the founder of www.clergyagainstbullets.org, co-founder of the Community Hevra Kadisha of Greater Boston, founder of Emunat HaLev: the Jewish Meditation and Mindfulness Institute of Temple Emunah, and served as a visiting scholar at Brandeis University.

Rabbi Adina Lewittes (Dini) is the founding rabbi of Sha'ar, a northern NJ/NYC-based, values-driven Jewish community oriented around the call to societal, environmental and spiritual sustainability. Sha'ar provides multiple gateways into Jewish life exemplified by a commitment to inclusiveness, diversity, innovation, scholarship, excellence and collaboration. Dini recently served as the Scholar in Residence at Congregation B'nai Jeshurun in NYC and is a member of the senior rabbinic faculty of the Shalom Hartman Institute. She also serves on the Board of Trustees of the Abraham Joshua Heschel School. Previously, Dini served as the Assistant Dean of the Rabbinical School at JTS, and founded a synagogue in Englewood, New Jersey, modelling shared leadership and collective communal responsibility. Dini regularly enjoys speaking engagements in the US and Canada and publishing essays on topics including Jewish identity, leadership, Jewish innovation, sexual/gender diversity, multifaith/multiheritage marriage and engagement, and contemporary Jewish spirituality. She is married to Andi Lewittes, and has four children, two stepchildren, and one incredible dog.

Rabbi Asher Lopatin is Excutive Director of the Community Jewish Relations Council (JCRC)/AJC of Detroit, and the founding director of the Detroit Center for Civil Discourse, a nonprofit designed to bring diverse people together in enriching dialogue, as well as the founding rabbi of Kehillat Etz Chayim, a new, Modern Orthodox synagogue in metropolitan Detroit. Prior to serving in these roles, he was president of Yeshivat Chovevei Torah Rabbinical School in New York and the senior rabbi of Anshe Sholom B'nai Israel Congregation in Chicago. While in Chicago, he and his wife, Rachel, helped found the pluralistic Chicago Jewish Day School and he co-chaired the Jewish Muslim Community Building Initiative of the Jewish Council on Urban Affairs. A Rhodes Scholar and Truman Fellow with an M. Phil in Medieval Arabic Thought from Oxford University, Rabbi Lopatin also has done doctoral work at St. Antony's College, Oxford, in Islamic Fundamentalist attitudes towards Jews and Israel. He received ordination from Rav Ahron Soloveichik and Yeshivas Brisk in Chicago, and from Yeshiva University, as a Wexner Graduate Fellow. In 2011, Rabbi Lopatin became a permanent member of The Council on Foreign Relations.

Rabbi Aaron Melman is the head rabbi of Congregation Beth Shalom in Northbrook, IL. Rabbi Melman served as a student chaplain with the New York City Fire Department (FDNY) and, since 2002, he has served the Northbrook Fire Department as its first and only chaplain. Rabbi Melman is involved in the community through the Northbrook Clergy Association, and serves on the Board of Directors of The Norton and Elaine Sarnoff Center for Jewish Genetics. He is a Past-President of the Chicago Region of Rabbinical Assembly and is a member of the Chicago Board of Rabbis. Rabbi Melman has also served as a guest lecturer over the past several years at the Chicago School of Professional Psychology.

Ruth Messinger was president of American Jewish World Service for 18 years and is currently the organization's first global ambassador. AJWS is the leading Jewish organization working to fight poverty and pursue justice in the developing world. Prior to AJWS, Messinger served as a City Council member in New York City and as Manhattan Borough President. A tireless advocate and social change visionary, Messinger mobilizes faith-based communities throughout the U.S. to promote human rights. She is also currently doing international human rights work for AIDS Free World and, in 2017, became the inaugural JTS Finkelstein Institute Social Justice Fellow.

Rabbi Sydney Mintz was ordained in 1997 by the Hebrew Union College-Jewish Institute of Religion in New York City. She is the founder of the award winning Late Shabbat Young Adult Program at Congregation Emanu-El where she has served as Rabbi for the past 23 years. Rabbi Mintz became a Senior Rabbinic Fellow at the Shalom Hartman Institute in Jerusalem in 2004 and serves on the National Board of Bend the Arc: A Jewish Partnership for Justice and on the 360Advisory Board of The

Reimagine End of Life Festival. She is the co-creator of the Book of Life Project with her beloved colleagues Rabbis Matthew Gewirtz and Yoshi Zweiback. In 2018, Rabbi Mintz's one woman show "You May Think I'm Funny, But It's Not" premiered and sold out at the Marsh Theatre in San Francisco. @RebSyd

Rabbi Avram Mlotek is a rabbi, cantor, writer, and actor. In 2015, he co-founded Base Hillel, a new model for Jewish practice that reaches out to unaffiliated young adults. Avram works as the rabbi for Base Hillel's Manhattan location and serves as director of spiritual life for the international Base program, as well as acting as rabbi in residence at the Marlene Meyerson JCC Manhattan. Follow him at avrammlotek.com, @avrammlotek on Instagram, and at @RabbiAvMlotek on Twitter.

Rabbi Jack Moline is President of Interfaith Alliance and a 1982 graduate of JTS.

Rabbi Joel Mosbacher is the senior rabbi of Temple Shaaray Tefila in New York City. Rabbi Mosbacher holds a Doctorate of Ministry with a focus on Pastoral Counseling from the Hebrew Union College-Jewish Institute of Religions, from which he was ordained in 1998. Rabbi Mosbacher is a social justice leader within the Reform movement. A recipient of the T'ruah Rabbinic Human Rights Hero Award in 2016, he serves on the national strategy team of the Metro Industrial Areas Foundation, and is a national co-chair of Metro-IAF's Do Not Stand Idly By campaign to reduce gun violence.

Rabbi Mosbacher has been featured in national news outlets, and he speaks and writes extensively on issues concerning social justice, Israel, and Jewish values, among others. Most recently, he is a contributing author to three publications from the Central Conference of American Rabbis (CCAR): *The Sacred Table: Creating a Jewish Food Ethic*, *Moral Resistance and Spiritual Authority*, and *The Sacred Exchange: Creating a Jewish Money Ethic*.

Rabbi Jesse M. Olitzky is senior rabbi and spiritual leader at Congregation Beth El in South Orange, New Jersey where he preaches and teaches about a Torah that demands of us to build a more just society. You can follow him on social media @JMOlitzky

Rabbi Dan Ornstein is rabbi at Congregation Ohav Shalom, a writer, and a Jewish day school teacher living in Albany, New York. He is the author of Cain v Abel: A Jewish Courtroom Drama (Jewish Publication Society 2020)

Rabbi Yael B. Ridberg serves as the spiritual leader of Congregation Dor Hadash in San Diego, California. In addition to her congregational responsibilities, Rabbi Ridberg serves on the Board of The San Diego Jewish Academy. She lives in La Jolla with her husband and four daughters.

Rabbi Jeffrey K. Salkin is the rabbi of Temple Israel in West Palm Beach, Florida, a prominent author, and a columnist for religionnews.com.

Rabbi Ezra Schwartz is a Rosh yeshiva and *bochein* (Official Examiner for Shiur placement exams at RIETS/YU) at Rabbi Isaac Elchanan Theological Seminary, an affiliate of Yeshiva University in New York City.

Rabbi David Spinrad is the rabbi of Beth El Hebrew Congregation in Alexandria, Virginia.

Rabbi Ravid Tilles serves as Director of Jewish Life and Learning at Solomon Schechter Day School of Greater Boston

Rabbi Rachel Timoner is a renowned rabbi, author and activist. She currently serves as Senior Rabbi at Congregation Beth Elohim in Brooklyn, New York and previously served as Associate Rabbi of Leo Baeck Temple in Los Angeles, California.

Rabbi Annie Tucker is the Senior Rabbi of Temple Israel Center in White Plains, NY, having previously served at Beth Hillel Bnai Emunah in Wilmette, IL (2013-2019) and The Jewish Center in Princeton, NJ (2006-2013).

Rabbi Jeremy Winaker has served in a variety of Jewish communal roles: as a pulpit rabbi, as University of Delaware Hillel's Senior Jewish Educator, as Albert Einstein Academy's Head of School, and more. His primary interest is in bringing Jewish Wisdom and people together wherever they may be. Ordained at the Jewish Theological Seminary of America, Rabbi Winaker also holds a BA with Honors in Philosophy from Swarthmore College. He is a Rabbis Without Borders Fellow. He has lived in Wilmington, DE with his family since 2009.

Rabbi David Wolkenfeld is the rabbi of Anshe Sholom B'nai Israel Congregation in Chicago.

Rabbi Jill Zimmerman, Founder & Spiritual Leader of Path with Heart, and Hineni: Your Path to Presence. Rabbi Zimmerman is an activist, author, and mindfulness teacher. She can be found at ravjill.com.

Jennifer Rudick Zunikoff is a storyteller, educator, poet, facilitator and coach based in Baltimore, Maryland. She is the founder, director, and storytelling coach of The Golden Door: Storytelling for Social Justice.

Made in the USA
Middletown, DE
07 January 2024

47407392R00124